Praise for Mile Markers

"Few writers are capable of pulling readers out of their seats and into an adventure quite like Robert. Every page oozes with a palpable joy for cycling, so much so I could practically feel 'Mile Markers' in my legs by the end."
—Joe Bauer, author of *Talking Tico*

"It's wonderful to find a book that fully expreses the personalty of its author. Robert Isenberg's book, Milemarkers compresses two cities, a father-son relationship, and the joy of pedaling into a truly enjoyable read. It's got a bright blue cover, too."
—Mark Binder, author of *The Groston Rules*

Mile Markers

ROBERT ISENBERG

First U.S. Edition 2024
10 9 8 7 6 5 4 3 2 1
ISBN: **9798879846713** Trade Paperback

Last Picked Books
Pittsburgh, PA

Printed in the United States of America

Jack London quote: "The Letters of Jack London: 1913-1916". Stanford University Press. Volume three, 1988.

Many of these essays were first published, in slightly different form, in other publications: "Killing the Messenger" in the book *The Legend of Pangkor*; "Riding Home" in *Sybarite*; "Ghost Bike" in *Belt*; "The World According to Thomas Stevens" in *Longreads*; "Jumped" in *East Side Monthly*; and "A Bicycle Built for Two," "The Magic Mountain," "When You Come to a Fork in the Road, Take It," "Keep Calm and Pedal On," "We're Jammin'," "Rein[forc]ing the Wheel," "Behold, the Kwiggle," "Rack 'Em," "Wheels of Freedom," "Bamboo Revolution," "If a Tree Falls in the Woods," "Paved with Good Intentions," "The Perspiration Paradox," "The Right Gear," "The Globe-Girdlers," "All Aboard!" and "Sole-Crusher" on Medium.

For my family.

CONTENTS

Introduction • 1
Killing the Messenger • 9
Riding Home • 16
A Bicycle Built for Two • 25
The Magic Mountain • 32
When You Come to a Fork in the Road, Take It • 38
Keep Calm and Pedal On • 44
We're Jammin' • 50
The World According to Thomas Stevens • 58
Rein[forc]ing the Wheel • 68
Behold, the Kwiggle • 76
Rack 'Em • 87
Wheels of Freedom • 94
Bamboo Revolution • 105
War Machine? • 114
If a Tree Falls in the Woods • 123
Paved with Good Intentions • 128
The Perspiration Paradox • 135
All Aboard! • 142
Ghost Bike • 147
Sole-Crusher • 157
Jumped • 168
The Globe-Girdlers • 176
Sit Back and Enjoy the Ride • 183
The Right Speed • 210

"Ever bike? Now that's something
that makes life worth living!"

- Jack London

INTRODUCTION

O̲ne winter morning, my son rides his bicycle for the first time.

"Can I ride my regular one?" Leo asks, pointing to the orange balance-bike leaning against our tool shed.

"Why don't you try the pedal-bike?" I say.

Leo pouts. "But I want to ride my *regular* one."

"Come *on*. Just give it a shot."

I roll the pedal-bike out of the garage. It's a clunky one-speed, painted electric blue. A decal across the top tube reads "Royal Baby," which I assume is just an awkward translation from Mandarin. The bike is stripped-down and cheap, but it has all the components Leo needs: crank arms, chain, brakes.

Leo clips his helmet under his chin. He climbs onto the plastic saddle. He gazes down the driveway. Concern fades from his face, eclipsed by determination. I pull out my phone. My thumb hovers over the "record" button. I have a good feeling about this one.

"Okay," I say. "Go ahead."

Leo presses down on a pedal. The wheels roll forward. He wobbles a little but stays upright. The bike passes some old lumber, our weathered picket fence, and continues down the pavement. His boots pump fluidly beneath him. He passes the lawn, the open gate, and coasts toward the side-walk.

"Okay—*stop!*"

He does. Just before drifting into the street, Leo squeezes the brake. He dismounts, hops on one foot, and whirls around. He still holds the handlebars. The bike remains in his grasp.

"*Perfect!*" I cry. "How do you feel?"

Leo waves. A childlike "all clear." And then, with a mittened hand, he shoots me a thumbs-up.

Rite of Passage

I play this video over and over. Of all the footage I've captured with my smartphone, this is my most cherished clip. Leo has pedaled a bike before. He's ridden the Royal Baby in figure-eights around the park. He knows what riding a bike *should* feel like. But he's never started and stopped on his own. He's never moved through space, unprotected by a nearby adult with outstretched hands. With each attempt, his interest fizzled. Then came December 30, 2020, at 12:15 p.m., the precise moment Leo first bicycled on his own.

Riding a bike is a major rite of passage, and there's no telling when it will happen. Most of us learn when we're young—too young to really remember, to understand what we've done. Training wheels disappear. Parents step into the sidelines. Suddenly, Leo is moving four times faster than he walks. He can do this all by himself. He *could* keep going, down the street, round the corner, into the next town. He knows his limits, sure. But to a seven-year-old, this is what freedom feels like. For the rest of his life, he will possess this mystical skill: balancing on two wheels and propelling himself for miles in any direction.

All winter, Leo rides his bike. The second the temperature rises to 50 degrees, we hit the pavement. We ride in circles around a parking lot. We ride down the local bike path. We ride a circuit around Roger Williams Park. Leo learns to keep right, to watch for cars, to anticipate branches and frost heaves. He chatters the whole time, telling me every thought in his head. He points out every squirrel. He marvels at graffiti on concrete walls. Under every bridge, he belts out a song, because he can't resist the echo.

And each time we ride together, my heart throbs with pride. He gets bolder, and I love to watch him navigate curves, conquer hills, share the road. Which is all great, of course. But even better is his spirit: Leo *absorbs* the landscape. He hears every chirp of every bird. He wonders how old this trestle bridge is. He asks which Native American nation once lived in these woods. He squeals to a stop, and he points at a log in the stream; there's a painted turtle sunning itself there, and it may be the greatest thing he's ever seen.

Lots of parents like to ride bikes with their kids. Lots of kids know how to live in the moment. But I, in particular, have really lucked out. Leo appreciates bikes in exactly the way I hoped he would. Leo has no idea how much this means to me.

Who Papa Is

To Leo, I am "Papa."

Papa is medium-sized, for a grownup. He has a reddish beard with patches of gray. He laughs a lot, mostly at his own jokes. Papa likes hiking in the woods. Papa likes to cook the family dinner each night. He likes reading books aloud and acting out all the characters' voices. Papa likes movies and Legos and drawing pictures. And yes, he likes to ride bikes.

Papa is always flying out the door with a helmet in hand. His U-lock and fingerless gloves are always lying around the house. In the garage, Leo sees several bicycles, of all shapes and sizes, plus tires and tubes and tools, but never an actual car. He knows that Papa has bicycled for a long time, like just about every grown-up. Papa plods along, taking in the sights; but every now and again, he accelerates, bombing down the trail at incredible speeds. He can do all sorts of crazy things on a bike, like hop a curb or ride with no hands. Papa knows exactly where to go—every street corner, every sign—and even when they get lost, Papa always finds a way back. Papa can fix anything; he adjusts the seat and pumps up the tires. When Leo's pedal falls off, Papa knows how to screw it back on.

Or so it all seems.

But as Leo grows up, he'll learn some things. He'll realize that Papa is a very average cyclist. Papa doesn't bike fast, even for a middle-aged man. He can't do *real* tricks, like flips off a ramp. He's never entered a single race. He knows only the most basic mechanics, like how to adjust brakes and patch a flat. Papa doesn't eat a special diet, and it shows. He doesn't have a training regimen. He makes tons of bone-headed mistakes. He's never ridden more than 70 miles in a single day.

(Leo, like all kids, will learn that his Papa is not a demigod, but merely a Papa).

But that's not all Leo will learn. Papa really *loves* cycling, far more than the standard-issue dad. It's perfectly normal for Papa to bike eight miles to work, every chance he gets. This, Leo will discover, isn't your typical commute. Papa reads book after book about cycling—histories, biographies, travel stories, anything he can get his hands on. Often, Papa will bike to the library to pick up books about biking. Papa watches movies about cycling. He reads blogs. He spends whole evenings online, window-shopping for new gear. Left to his own devices, Papa might not flip on a TV for weeks; but he could watch cyclists on YouTube all day long.

Leo will learn that not every Papa hates driving a car. Hates it so much, Papa let his driver's license expire and simply refused to drive—*for eight years*. This was all before Leo was born, so he never saw Papa trudge uphill through Pittsburgh rainstorms on a rusty seven-speed. He never knew Papa as a twenty-something bohemian, living in a dumpy apartment with two roommates, owning little more than a bed and a bike. He has no idea Papa bought his first car at the age of 34, and only as a last resort. It will take Leo a long time to conclude that this is not normal dad behavior, and that Papa is kind of a kook.

Not until they ride together in the streets of Providence does Leo understand how comfortable Papa is in frenzied urban traffic. Papa doesn't let a bunch of cars push him around. Story by story, Leo will piece together the breadth of Papa's travels—his bike tours across Costa Rica; along the coast of Taiwan; down the Great Allegheny Passage; through the French countryside and Rhine River Valley; in South-western deserts and Asian rainforests. Sweating down rough roads in foreign countries is not how most Papas spend their free time. And *this* is how Papa can navigate invisible shoulders, narrowly missing side-view mirrors, swaddled in exhaust and pelted with pebbles. Papa doesn't like traffic, but he knows how to handle it. No matter how snarled the gridlock, Papa has always seen worse.

Eventually, Leo will find that even these oddities aren't *that* odd. Leo himself will graduate to gears, shocks, and drop-bars. He'll master right-of-way, and then he'll cruise the 'hood with all his bros. He'll see how normal all this is. Plenty of Papas obsess over cycling. Some are far *more* obsessive, never mind faster and more athletic. Some Papas spend a fortune on custom rides; they pedal a thousand miles every month. Leo's Papa is nothing like that, and probably never will be.

But there's one thing Papa does that stands out. Something almost nobody does: *he writes about cycling.*

Late at night, as Papa lounges on the sofa, tapping at his phone, he's actually adding sentences to a Google Doc. When he stares into space, Papa is contemplating bicycles and how to describe them. These sentences turn into articles, and the articles pop up in newspapers and magazines. One day, it will dawn on Leo just how much Papa has written about this singular machine—stories and essays, guides and profiles, book chapters and even poems. Leo may never read a word of it, but he will know, as time goes by, how much gray matter Papa dedicated to his muse. Leo will find, to his delight—or maybe horror—that much of that writing is also about him.

Because Papa has an unwavering faith in the power of

the bicycle. The older Papa gets, the stronger his conviction. The bicycle isn't just sports equipment, or a fun hobby, or cheap transportation. To Papa, a bicycle is the purest innovation, a tool of liberation, the antidote for a million human woes. When Papa pedals down the way, the sensation is sacred to him. He's going somewhere. He's alive.

At last, Leo will find this book. Flipping through these very pages, he will travel the same roads—and paths, and sidewalks—that his Papa has. He will discover the same obsessions, meet the same dreamers, assess the same inventions, and puzzle out the same problems. As the years pass, and the role of bicycles evolves in public life, these stories will remain frozen in time, a portrait of a particular man in a particular era. At my age, Leo will compare his world to mine; the things that changed; the things that stayed the same. Like mile markers on the trail, these vignettes are intended to remind us where we are, how far we've come, and how far we've got to go.

And to keep enjoying ourselves—because what else is it all for?

Part 1:
Tune-Ups

KILLING THE MESSENGER

It was all about speed, that summer.

Gulping coffee. Tapping my heel. Hearing my cell phone ring. Scribbling down addresses. Hopping on my bike. Diving into traffic. Dodging cars in the narrow streets. Signing into an office building. Picking up a parcel. Racing somewhere else. Handing it off to a receptionist. Swigging from a Nalgene. Repeat, repeat, repeat.

The memory is a blur, but so was the job. Asphalt and brick. Plate-glass and decorative bushes. Mini Coopers and Ryder trucks. And everywhere, crowds of people. They lumbered down sidewalks, yelled into phones, swished through revolving doors. Some wore do-rags and jerseys. Others wore blouses, ties, polished shoes. All these costumes blended in the streets of downtown Pittsburgh, looking just right. All of them belonged here.

But not me.

I was the outlier—the guy wearing cargo shorts and a sweat-soaked T-shirt. The guy affixing his bicycle to a lamppost with a gangly wire-lock. I dripped onto waxed lobby floors. The single strap of my messenger bag cut a diagonal line across my chest. My reddish hair looked like swamp grass. My shoes split at the seams. I wore a visored helmet most of the day, and each time I whipped it off, it jangled from a carabiner. Every few blocks, I wiped the fog from my sunglasses. All day, I smelled like an old sock.

Still, I *loved* being a bike messenger. I couldn't believe I had the chance to do this—to carry packages through the breakneck traffic of the Golden Triangle, to literally bike for money. I was twenty-five, dead broke, and had nothing to lose. I couldn't stomach another temp job. I'd entered more data into more spreadsheets than anyone ever should. I was squirrelly and lost, and I needed, more than anything, to stretch my legs, to pedal my way through a scorching Pennsylvania summer. If I had to hit rock bottom, I might as well hit it as hard as I could.

The Ad

The ad in the newspaper said, "MAKE LOTS OF $$$." I circled the ad with a pen and added some exclamation points. I'd heard of bike couriers, of course. Now and then, I spotted them on the avenue—tall guys in minimalist outfits, leaning into their drop-bars with all their might.

Did they really make "$$$"? If so, where had this job been all my life?

Four years had passed since I'd graduated college. My career as a freelance writer had been a rollercoaster, and for now that ride was closed for repairs. My commissions had dried up. My laptop barely switched on. I couldn't afford an internet connection, so I visited the Carnegie Library and used the computers for 45-minute stretches. I lived with two friends but could barely afford my $200 monthly rent. I slurped down ramen noodles and canned soups. I had no insurance of any kind. I couldn't remember the last time I'd visited a dentist, much less a doctor.

Worst of all, I didn't own a car. I knew *how* to drive, but I hated doing it. As the years slipped by, my original license expired, and I shrugged it off. *So what?* I thought. *I'll take the bus.*

I'd backed myself into a corner—no car, no suit, no practical experience. Nobody wanted some kid with a degree in journalism, magna cum laude or otherwise. Not even the local warehouse would hire me.

But I had a bicycle. A hybrid with twenty-one gears and durable tires. And I knew how to ride it.

I made the call.

The man on the other end said, "How soon can you get here?"

Money in the Bank

I had trouble finding the company headquarters. The building stood in a quiet industrial park, a maze of corrugated steel walls and dormant forklifts, and the door was marked by one small sign: "National Shipping."

The office was filled with empty desks and standing fans. A CB radio crackled in the corner. Ashtrays were everywhere.

The man who welcomed me was Del, a soft-spoken man with a mustache. We shook hands, and he held out a contract and some tax forms. The interview was brief.

"We split the deliveries fifty-fifty," said Del. "Once you make a delivery, we give you a confirmation number, and that's money in the bank."

Money in the bank, I thought. *Drop stuff off, cha-ching!* I practically frothed.

"What kind of training?" I asked.

Del shook his head. "No training. You just *go*."

There were only three requirements: I had to use my own cell phone, my own bag, and my own bike. I'd also have to sign a waiver, because I was an independent contractor, and none of this was insured. Also, my first payment wouldn't be processed for 10 business days; but after that, I could expect a weekly paycheck.

Plus, I could take breaks whenever I wanted. Or even call off a whole day.

Perfect, I thought. *Just what I've been looking for.*

Treks and the City

And so, I biked.

I biked between cars, over potholes, through lightning storms. Down dark alleys. I biked on the sidewalk, in the bus lane, the wrong way down one-way streets. Through puddles left by open hydrants and over more bridges than I could count. Through more red lights than I could count. As fast as I could, all day, for days on end, I biked.

And I savored it all, because I loved Pittsburgh. I loved the jumbled streets, the mismatched façades, the sultry summer air. I loved swerving past car doors and delivery trucks, panhandlers and jaywalkers, the claustrophobic confusion all around me. I hurtled down this deadly gauntlet, knuckles white against my handlebars. Somehow, this all made sense. The dangers were blunt and never-ending. I had no one to rely on but myself. It was me against the world, and I'd taken that fight outside, where it belonged.

The thing is, I'm a very friendly person. *Unsettlingly* friendly. I smile all the time. When I'm not chuckling, I'm laughing. With each delivery, I barged into an office building, and the security guard recoiled. There I was, a glistening, disheveled young man with lobster-red forearms and flopping shoelaces, beaming like a maniac.

"Afternoon!" I'd exclaim. "Nice to see the sun out, isn't it? Got a delivery for the thirty-second floor!"

I signed my name in dozens of ledgers, the ink smearing beneath my clammy hand. I shared elevators with businessmen in suits and gelled hair. Jovial conversation stopped the second I stepped aboard. The men looked away, cleared their throats.

"How about that Pirates game?" I'd say, and everyone would mumble in agreement—even though I hadn't actually seen a Pirates game in years.

I kept smiling, even as I gritted my teeth, because I *needed* this—to pick up envelopes and move them from one place to another. I woke up craving the humid air and burn of lactic acid. In motion, I could forget about the crumbling economy, the ongoing wars in the Middle East, the Patriot Act, the school shootings. All that mattered was my bike, this trusty machine, and the yardage between us and our destination. Speed was everything. Speed, and staying alive.

Dealbreaker

I opened my first paycheck with trembling fingers. The paper was thick and the perforations difficult to tear. At last, the numbers revealed themselves. I stared, shocked.

Eighty-five dollars.

Over the course of thirty-five hours—pumping the pedals as hard as I could, dodging accidents at every turn—I had earned eighty-five dollars. *Before taxes.*

I slumped into my couch. For once, I didn't laugh, or chuckle, or even smile. All that work, for *this*. Not even minimum wage. Not even *half* of minimum wage. Money in the bank, sure, just as Del had promised. But nothing I would call "$$$."

The truth was, National Shipping wasn't really a "bike courier service." Most of their deliveries were made by car, which was probably more lucrative. Bikes were just a bonus. A way to diversify.

Just like that, the dream dissolved. I would never be a bike messenger. And maybe that was fine. You win some, you lose some.

Generation Rickshaw

Years have passed since I opened that paycheck. The world has changed in ways I could never have imagined back in the summer of 2005. My roommate installed something called "WiFi" in our apartment. I opened a MySpace account. My friend showed me something called a "smartphone." On TV, the real estate market imploded. Barack Obama was elected president. Friends talked me into signing up for Facebook, whatever that was. I went to graduate school. I bought a townhouse. I married my then-girlfriend. I inherited my first iPhone. I sent my first Tweet. I got a new driver's license. I bought my first car.

And then, out of nowhere, Uber existed. Followed by Lyft, Postmates, and InstaCart. The world was suddenly crawling with amateur messengers, carrying people and goods from place to place. Friends enlisted as drivers, picking up strangers at all hours of day and night. My own brother became a bike courier in New York, riding thousands of miles through Manhattan gridlock. Every Christmas, people I knew signed up as Amazon drivers. The job that had seemed so brazen when I was twenty-five years old was now a regular side-hustle. If you aren't moving stuff around in your spare time, you're hiring other people to move stuff around in *their* spare time.

I won't go back, of course. I loved that bicycle, but it's long gone, along with that whole way of being. I'm no longer a twenty-something, kicking and screaming in the urban jungle. I'll use a bike for all kinds of things, just not to make a living.

But the legacy lives on. I pedal through the city, and I think back to that kaleidoscopic time. If I could have earned a living wage, how long would it have lasted? Months? Years? Would I still be doing it? Who would I be?

RIDING HOME

PICTURE YOURSELF ON Main Street, a quiet road with old brick factories and weird intersections. It's right next to your new office. This is where you start. You're seated on your bike, balancing with your foot against a curb. This is your first ride in Rhode Island, where you now live. Your lunch break just started, but you've already eaten a can of noodle soup at your desk. You now have a whole hour to yourself.

Launch forward. Pedal up a narrow street, then cross Pawtucket Avenue, wary of distracted drivers. Pass rows of clapboard houses. Turn right on Hope.

"Hope" is a word you'll hear a lot. Soon you'll learn that this one word is the state motto. "Hope" is sewn into the state flag. There's a Mount Hope, and also a Mount Hope Bridge. Now you're rolling down Hope Street, a major artery through Providence. You'll soon hear a joke—actually, you'll read it on a novelty T-shirt—that "rich folks live on Power Street, but most of us live off Hope."

Imagine a long, gentle hill. Big houses, nice lawns. Stores emerge, then restaurants—a little business district. Gift shops, a toy shop, a shop that sells only olive oil. Soon, you will eat lunch at *that* Indian restaurant; you will slurp ramen at *that* Japanese place. You will snicker at the sign, "Rochambeau Library," because you only know the name "Rochambeau" as a pseudonym for "Rock, Paper, Scissors." In time, you will learn about the famous French general who helped win the American Revolution, and you will carry armloads of books through this library's doors.

Hall Pass

Now imagine that time passes: weeks and months. Each lunch break, you push your bike out of your cubicle and into a third-floor elevator. Excitement builds as you jog through the lobby. Outside, you propel yourself into traffic and pedal hard through the backstreets of Providence. Venture a mile farther each time. Commit new landmarks to memory—the deli, the yoga studio, the stone church.

Coast down the single lane of Thayer Street, where students crowd the sidewalks and emerge from grab-and-go eateries. Make a circle around the iron gates and brick walls of Brown University. Glide along the scenic curves of Wickenden Street, with its cafes and antique shops and century-old hardware store.

Block by block, throw yourself at the city.

The First Time, Once More

Assume you've moved a lot in your life. You've done this many times before—arrived in a neighborhood and known nothing about it. Everything was fresh and novel. Each time, you studied the new environs from a bicycle saddle. No place ever made sense until you explored it on two wheels. Names are just names until you've sweated through them, dodged their traffic, hit their dead-ends. You need the air and elements, the potholes and yield signs. As a kid, this is how you learned the gravel roads of your hometown. As a wide-eyed college student, a bike was how you puzzled out the fragmented hills of Pittsburgh. As a new father, a bike was how you cobbled together the dusty municipalities of Phoenix. Most recently, a bike was how you tried to untangle the cartographic knots of Boston—and, for the first time, failed.

Now you're here. Married. A family man. Nearly 40 years old. You live in Rhode Island, and you're digging in. No more moving vans. No more reassembling dining room sets. You never again want to call the gas company to have your service switched on. This is the last stop. This is *it*.

You have mixed feelings about this. You may never explore a new home for the first time, which is strange to think. But this is the land you want to *keep* exploring for years to come. One block at a time, you'll know this city—this whole state—as well as they can possibly be known.

Run That Past Me Again

Providence confuses you—at first. Why is there an East *Side* and a West *End?* Why isn't Wayland Square shaped anything like a square? Is that seriously how you pronounce *Pawtucket?* Why is it called *India Point* and not *Indian Point*, which would make so much more sense? What's the difference between *East Providence* and *the East Side of Providence?* What's that, you say? East Side is a neighborhood and East Providence is a whole separate city, even though they're only separated by a bridge? *Really?*

But your bicycle accelerates your understanding. You ride between the skyscrapers of Downcity, across the outdoor bus depot of Kennedy Plaza, and through the old Mafia stomping grounds of Federal Hill. You sew it all together in your mind. You glide beneath an archway and admire the pineapple dangling from its center, because Rhode Islanders cherish pineapples as a symbol of hospitality. Later you're corrected: the sculpture isn't a pineapple at all, but a pine cone.

You start with the landmarks you notice on your rides, but you gradually exchange these for the landmarks locals actually care about. The deco magnificence of the Superman Building. The hard-to-find gravestone of H.P. Lovecraft. The face of a scowling warrior carved into a stone façade, known to everyone as the "Turk's Head." A hilltop statue of Roger Williams, the free-spirited Puritan who founded Providence; not only had you never heard of Roger Williams, but you spend months calling him William Rogers. From your speeding bike, you spot rowing shells in the bay and Venetian-style gondolas in the river. You marvel that such a small city can have so many sights.

You come to admire the Crook Point Bascule Bridge, a steel-framed drawbridge that rises into the air like the head of a brontosaurus. The beams are caked in rust and graffiti; where the bike path crosses old railroad tracks, a fence has been erected, but trespassers have clearly peeled back the chain link and freely roam the industrial ruins. The bridge was raised in 1976 and never let down again, a monument frozen in time.

Nobody's Perfect

You make mistakes, of course.

You ride the wrong way down one-way streets. You get so lost in the West End that you have to stop every few blocks to consult GPS. You ride over a jagged chunk of metal and your tire whizzes flat. You take a patch of ice too fast and topple sideways, knocking the wind out of yourself.

These are small, silly accidents. But you ride farther, and your mistakes get more intense.

Like the first time you spot Blackstone Boulevard, in the corner of your eye. You can't believe what you're looking at: one road goes one way, another road goes the opposite way, and in the middle is a mile-long vertical park. On each road, there's a crisply painted bike lane; a dirt path bisects the park. What is this magical place, just a few blocks from your office? How have you never noticed this before?

Then you brake. Hard. You got so excited by the bike lanes, you nearly rear-ended a Honda Civic.

Time passes.

On Reservoir Avenue, you pedal down a narrow shoulder, past a row of idling cars. Just as the light turns green, a pickup turns right—no signal—and nearly plows through you.

More time passes.

On Terrace Street, you hit another red light. You want to turn, so you maneuver into the left lane. Cars queue up behind you. One is a beat-up sedan with cardboard over the rear windows. A man leans out.

"Where's your fuckin' plate, man?"

You think he's talking to somebody else. Why would he be talking to you? But then you hear him, louder: "I said,

Where's you're fuckin' plate, asshole?"

And you realize he means *you.* He means you have no license plate. You're not a car, so you don't belong on the road. His engine revs. The light turns green, and you pump as fast as you can. You have no idea what this guy will do. Nudge you off the road? Chuck a bottle at your head? So you charge for the sidewalk. Your tire thumps up a curb-cut, and you angle your handlebars around a lamppost.

The old car roars away. All you see is an outstretched arm, and its outstretched middle finger.

One near-miss at a time, you identify the bad spots. Whatever doesn't kill you makes you smarter.

As Luck Would Have It

You think to yourself: *I wonder if Rhode Island has bike paths? Wouldn't that be nice!*

Little do you know, Rhode Island is *full* of paved trails. When you finally bother to find them, you're gobsmacked by how smooth they are. This isn't the crushed limestone you're accustomed to. Not just that: of all the places you've lived, *no* city has ever had trails as nice as these.

First you try the Washington Secondary Bike Path, and you lose yourself in suburban woods. The level pavement goes on and on. You bike across trestle bridges, under highways, over rivers and ponds. The development fades away, and you realize you're in the countryside. You pass farms and forests. You can't believe the smallest state in the nation could extend so far. After 19 miles, the trail wanes and ends. You consult a digital map and realize you've nearly reached the Connecticut border. The trail cuts a continuous line across half the state.

You find more trails. Seven miles along the Woonasquatucket River. Ten miles along the Blackstone River. Fourteen miles along the rocky coast of Narragansett Bay. Two-and-a-half miles across Quonset. Seven miles through the villages of South County. A three-mile circle around the ballfields and beaches of Warwick City Park. The tarmac is buttery. Crisp lines run down the middle, dividing lanes of traffic. Joggers nod as they bounce past. Cyclists wear Lycra, fleece, camouflage, sundresses. They come in all ages and sizes. Tricycles squeak and ebikes hum. Fishing poles jut out of backpacks. Fathers haul carriers full of babies. A stereo is mounted on handlebars and blasts hip-hop into the ether. The East Bay Bike Path is like a superhighway. People actually use this path to get places, and for every other conceivable reason.

It dawns on you, slowly but surely, how lucky you are to live here.

Building the Cycling City

But there's more. Just when you start to know where you're going—and you can basically get to, say, your son's swim lessons without using Google Maps—the bike lanes pop up.

Mayor Jorge Elorza, it turns out, is an avid cyclist. He's been pushing for bike lanes for years, long before you bumbled into town. And he's hardly the first; local advocates are fierce, you discover. If they had their way, Providence would transform into Copenhagen. The slender streets would flood with bicycles. The highways would drain themselves of cars. The smog would dissipate. The automotive din would quiet, leaving only human voices and the occasional barking dog.

You think, *Right on. Absolutely. That's my kind of Kool-Aid!*

Painted lanes appear. Plastic dividers sprout from the pavement. Parking spaces cheat left. You follow signs and arrows from one segment to the next. Piece by piece, the new map falls into place. You discover a secret ramp, which takes you underneath Providence Place Mall. You safely climb Clifford Street over all eight lanes of Interstate 95. Broad Street, a long boulevard known mostly for fast food restaurants and occasional gunshots, opens a bike lane running 1.5 miles. In the months after it opens, you ride this route over and over, memorizing storefronts you never knew existed.

So, you're not just lucky to live here; you're lucky to live here *now*. Your arrival is an accident of fate, but somehow, you've arrived in the middle of a cycling renaissance. Providence *isn't* Copenhagen. You doubt it ever will be. But holy mackerel, what wondrous things are happening.

Bonus Rounds

In time, you may think you've seen it all. You've biked every trail, then you bike every trail again. You know the slight variations in incline. You know when you'll shift gears. You anticipate—and judge—every road-crossing. You know when the turtles bury their eggs on the banks of the Blackstone River. You know where the South County Trail turns into a street, and when the trail resumes. You've covered every mile you can cover, you think.

But you're wrong, every time. You still surprise yourself.

You find a paved trail into Worcester. Another one out of New Bedford. A gravel rail-trail along the Massachusetts border. Dirt paths around parks and ponds. And behind the trail, there are always motorways—more bikeable roads than you know what to do with. You ride across the state in one day, from a cemetery in Woonsocket to a beach in Newport. Still, you have so much more to see, in every season and weather pattern. Alone or in duos or packs. On asphalt and macadam and cobblestone. The road goes on and on, and so do you.

A Bicycle Built for Two

I DON'T PLAN to prop my son on the back of my bicycle. It just kind of happens.

"Hey, Papa," says Leo, approaching the back of my Trek hybrid. "Can I get up there?"

At first I think he means the seat. He's climbed up here before, leaning into the handlebars and squeezing the brakes as I hold onto the frame. At six years old, he's much too small to reach the pedals, so the position is novel, like putting him in the driver's seat of our car.

But Leo doesn't mean the seat; he meant the luggage rack, a foot-long platform that hovers above my rear wheel.

"Well," I hedge. "I'm not sure if, uh—"

As usual, I can't stop him. Leo lifts himself onto the rack and straddles it. He looks at me expectantly. His eyes say, *Okay. Let's go.*

We're near the end of a bike ride through the East Side of Providence, on a fresh new trail that starts in India Point Park and skirts the Seekonk River. Leo has pushed himself down the trail on his "balance bike," a model with no pedals that helps kids bypass training wheels. We've gone a good distance, and in a mile or so, we'll be back at the car. This is

April, at the height of the coronavirus lockdown, and we've passed only a handful of daring souls.

Well, why not? I think. *Let's see if this works.*

To my surprise, it works great. Leo grabs my belt, and I pedal us slowly down the smooth asphalt. Leo giggles with joy. The breeze elates him. I'm surprised how easily we balance together, how secure he feels.

"Papa, can you go faster?" Leo coaxes.

So I pedal faster. We coast down a small hill and ascend another. We're back at the car in no time.

"What do you think?" I ask Leo.

"Can we do that again?"

I laugh. This stunt may have been fun, but it's not exactly safe. "Maybe," I say.

Whatever Works

Naturally, we do it again.

Quarantine is cruel to an outdoorsy father and his outdoorsy son, and after months of weathering a New England winter, the last thing I want is to squander a sunny afternoon.

But most public parks are closed. Shops and restaurants are shuttered. During my weekly visits to the supermarket, signs and stickers and billboards all command, STAY HOME. One bleak day, I drive across the state to take Leo to his favorite seascape, Black Point Trail. When we arrive, the parking lots are barricaded. I soon learn that every beach and playground is closed as well. Squad cars patrol the coast, enforcing the governor's mandate. I don't object, because I know all this was for my own health and safety. But I'm crestfallen all the same.

Only one green space remains open, to my shock and delight: the bike trails. Rhode Island is home to a superlative trail network, with routes as long as nineteen miles. This is an incredible feat for a state that's only fifty miles across. A month into the lockdown, *social distancing* feels heavy on the "distance." I need fresh air, activity, movement—and so does Leo.

"Hey, do you want to bike with me?" I ask the second the temperature hits fifty degrees.

"Um... maybe?" Leo responds, bouncing up and down on the trampoline that used to be our easy chair. "Can I ride on the back of your bike?"

This is a hard deal to turn down. Leo is too big for his balance bike; the seat is adjusted as far up as it will go. And he could—technically—operate his pedal bike. I've watched him ride, unassisted, around an entire baseball diamond. But he hates to start and stop. I find myself launching him forward, then running behind, breathlessly assuring him that he won't fall, just keep going. And then, instead of braking, he just falls sideways, and I'm forced to catch him. The process leaves us both exhausted.

So I relent. I let him ride on my luggage rack. He grips my belt loops for support. First we take little jaunts around the neighborhood. Then we roll into the next neighborhood. Over a significant hill. Onto the local bike path. One afternoon, we pedal eight miles along the Washington Secondary Trail. Hikers smile. Cyclists give me a thumbs up. Teenagers on BMX bikes point and cry, "Dude, that's awesome! Check out that kid!"

Leo basks in their attention. "Do they think I'm so cool?" he asks, with lovable sincerity.

"I think they do," I called over my shoulder.

"Why do they think I'm so cool?"

"Because you're doing something they don't usually see."

"Nobody does this? I'm the only one?"

"Yep. You're the only one."

And there's a reason for that, of course. Kindergartners aren't *supposed* to balance precariously on the luggage platforms of their fathers' bicycles, careening down rail-trails at twelve miles per hour. One spill could mean a broken wrist, a concussion, an endless visit to a COVID-infected ER. I love riding together, but I need to gear up. What we need is a ride-along.

Third Wheel

I know—I *should* just make him ride the bicycle. If he can already balance, why impede his progress? He could master pushing off and braking in a week or two. What's the point of throwing a wrench in the gears?

And why should I spend hours on Facebook Marketplace, combing through ads for a special one-wheeled bike that attaches to a larger bike? What compels me—in the middle of a pandemic—to drive to the next county, find the workshop of a man I'd never met, fork over sixty dollars in cash, and drive home with a used ride-along, without so much as a test-ride? Do I really expect Leo to just jump on this rusty contraption and hightail it down the road with me? Won't we look ridiculous, tethered together and hobbling along on three mismatched wheels?

As it happens, *I* was a late-blooming cyclist. Like Leo, I was terrified of falling. Unlike Leo, I clung to training wheels for years, artificially held up for all to see. My parents love to describe my metamorphosis: stubbornly refusing to bike on my own, no matter how many times my Dad took me to a local parking lot to practice. And then, one unremarkable day, I just *did it.* "We just had to wait for you to be ready," my Dad likes to say. "And then you just took off. And that was it."

I'm banking on Leo doing the same. Leo is a far braver boy than I was, more willing to try something scary; but when he *doesn't* want to, he knows how to drag his feet. Pedaling a bike will come, and I picture an adolescent Leo doing flips off half-pipes, or dive-bombing down mountains, or inching across continents with his old man. But there's no rush.

For now, Leo mounts the ride-along. He sinks into a plush, oversized seat. He clutches the handlebars like a Hell's Angel revving his hog. We launch forward, and I'm amazed how easily we float down the street. I tug him along, adjusting to the extra weight.

"Papa, are we going so fast?"

"I'd say we're going about ten miles per hour," I answer.

"Ohhh!" Leo exclaims, not having any idea what that means. "We're going *so fast!*"

We ride through nearby neighborhoods. We merge with the trail. We pass familiar shops and houses. With each landmark, Leo squeals with recognition; he can't believe how these isolated reference points connect to each other, an endless matrix of roads and sidewalks and paths. From a car window, the landscape is just a blur; now, he sees the natural progression of streets and houses, parks and bridges, donut shops and schools.

Over the next few months, we ride more than a hundred miles together, all over Rhode Island. We stop to spot wildlife by an old canal; we hold picnics in the grass. We lean against old masonry to gaze at waterfalls. Leo rides side-saddle, putting his full weight on a single pedal like a Cossack horseman—a trick that drives my wife crazy. When I stand up on my pedals to charge up a hill, so does Leo. He never complains about the view, even though my own body obstructs it. We love to pass other families, who wave to us and exclaim, "We have to get one of *those*."

As we coast down the East Bay Bike Path, skirting the rocky coast beneath a flawless blue sky, I wonder whether I would have done all this without COVID. Sitting at home, furloughed, forbidden long walks, the bike path keeps me sane. We kill hours driving to and from a trailhead, the bikes vibrating on our flimsy car rack; but each trip reveals to Leo how much cycling means to me. Locked into the same mechanism, he can see exactly what I see—the same scenery, scrolling past us at the same speed. Instead of explaining the rules of the road, Leo can watch me signal, stop, nod to drivers, slow and turn at intersections. The lessons are wordlessly programmed into his mind and body. Mile by mile, he *feels* this two-wheeled instruction. He does everything I do, and it's as easy as—well, you know.

Take the Wheel

But there's one surprise. Something I don't anticipate. The ride-along has its own pedals, so Leo can pump his legs as we go. I assume these pedals are useless; as long as I'm the one propelling us along, Leo doesn't have to flex a single muscle. He can't break or steer; in reality, the ride-along is just a glorified rickshaw.

Or is it?

One afternoon, Leo and I ride down the trail, and I stop pedaling. The terrain is flat; the wheels roll effortlessly. Then I felt a slight acceleration. Like the power-assist feature on an e-bike, pushing us forward. I crane my neck—and there's Leo, pedaling as hard as he can. His head is bowed with concentration. I can't even see his face beneath his helmet.

"Leo!" I cry. "Do you see what you're doing?"

"I'm moving us?" he huffs back, clearly already aware.

"You're moving us! Do you want me to help? Or do you want to keep going?"

"Keep... going..." he pants.

And so he does. For half a mile, Leo is our engine. My own legs relax. We're *really* moving. Leo sputters with exertion and triumph. For years, Leo has been driven places, walked places; accompanied and escorted and guided; handed off, from parent to teacher to babysitter to swim coach and back. Like every six-year-old, all Leo has ever known is a relay-race of parental supervision.

But not today. Today he's pedaling on his own. He goes as fast as he physically can. And it's Leo, not me, who takes us where we need to go.

The Magic Mountain

"HEY, YOU WANT to go biking?" I ask my son, one unseasonably warm winter day.

"Where?" he demands.

"Well, we could go to the park. Or we could take the bike trail..."

Leo sighs. "Papa, no offense, but I don't want to bike on those. They're a little bit—boring?"

"Okay. Where would you want to bike?"

"I sorta want to bike on *dirt*."

"Oh. You mean—mountain biking?"

"Yeah, mountain biking," says Leo, as if I've finally guessed the correct answer.

"Well, we could try some, uh, mountain biking..."

"Okay."

"Let me just, uh, find out where we can, uh, do that."

"Okay."

"Okay..." And I leave the room, to go consult the Internet. Truthfully, I have no idea where to go mountain biking in Rhode Island—or anywhere else, for that matter. Because somehow, I've never actually *gone* mountain biking.

MTB Prude

This is absurd, of course. I grew up in Vermont, which has some of the most beloved MTB trails in the country. Cycling is a major part of my life and identity. I can think of a dozen friends who are skilled mountain bikers, the kinds of people who ramble down single-tracks, launch off jumps, and "get mad air."

But I've never done it myself. When I think of biking, I think of bike lanes and asphalt paths, dirt roads and country highways. In Pittsburgh, the trails are largely paved with crushed limestone, and potholes and fallen branches are common; but this hardly compares to a rocky trench sliced into a hillside, punctuated with wood ramps. I will bike any road and hike any wilderness, but never have these pastimes met.

Honestly, I'm intimidated. The only mountain biking I've ever seen was on video, and these videos feature some of the best mountain bikers in the world. I like to call this "expert bias": you assume that, on the very first day, you'll have to do flips off a two-story cliff. After all, that's what people do on YouTube, usually to the rhythm of death metal.

Most people don't do that, of course. Much of mountain biking is just a sped-up version of hiking. Ascents can be laboriously slow, pedaled in very low gears. And riders don't have to hurl themselves down jagged escarpments. Indeed, rookies probably shouldn't.

We are rookies. We can take it slow. And if we hate it, at least we'll know.

Fellow Travelers

Freeway leads to road, then a smaller road, then an even smaller road, until my Subaru is deeply buried in the woodlands of Kent County. There's scarcely a human to be seen, except driving the occasional pickup. When we finally park in a gravel lot, a sign warns us not to cross a nearby fence, because it's a rifle range.

"I guess this is it," I say, killing the engine.

This is our first-ever visit to the Big River Management Area, an 8,000-acre preserve in West Greenwich. I'll later learn that Big River has a controversial history: back in the 1960s, residents were forcibly uprooted so that Rhode Island could make it a reservoir. But the land was never flooded; instead, Big River is a forest habitat and recreational area. If you look close, you can see traces of razed houses. But for the most part, there are gentle hills and deciduous forest as far as we can see.

We don't own real mountain bikes. Leo has a sturdy model with thick tires, but there's one rear brake and it has no gear shift. The small wheels can roll over anything, but only if he pedals as hard as he can. My bike is a Trek hybrid with delicate tires. Neither of us has shocks or suspension of any kind. Bringing our bikes to woodsy single-track is like bringing a Prius to a monster truck rally.

We venture down the main trail, which cuts a wide corridor through the forest. A steel gate is drawn over the entrance, but the "trail" clearly doubles as a road, probably for maintenance vehicles. The ground is sandy and soft, and we struggle to roll our way into the park.

"This is hard," Leo huffs. He loses traction again and again, only to push his bike like a scooter. I'm not faring much better. The terrain feels moist; I wonder for the thousandth time what it's like to ride on fat tires.

A half-mile later, we hit an intersection, where two narrow trails meander in opposite directions.

"Here we go," I say. "Your pick. Which way?"

Leo picks right, and we pedal onto a firm forest floor. We bounce over rocks and roots, up a gradual incline.

Another biker emerges from the trees. He wears a windbreaker and Spandex leggings. His helmet and backpack cling ergonomically to his body. He rides—of course—an *actual* mountain bike. The nubbed tires adhere to the path like Velcro. All his gear has a space-age cleanliness, as if it's been freshly picked from the racks of L.L. Bean.

"We're mountain biking!" Leo proclaims.

The man stops. He looks at my son through his gray-tinted Oakleys. He smiles, a warm smile made all the warmer by his salt-and-pepper scruff.

"It was hard before, because the ground was really soft, but now we're in the woods, and we're going higher up, and we're going to explore the whole forest!" Leo continues to the complete stranger.

"Yeah!" exclaims the rider. "It's a great day for a ride!"

"Sorry to stop you," I say, "but this is our first time here. Any etiquette we should know about?"

"Not really. The paths are all two-way. Right of way is to people going up. What else? Watch yourself around—" he names a trail that I instantly forgot. "Folks really barrel down that one."

Leo looks at me. His expression says, *I don't know what barreling means, but I know I want to do it.*

We thank the rider. The man stands up on his pedals, rising up the hill. Then he calls over his shoulder, "Have fun!"

Leo turns to me. "He was a really nice guy. I hope we see him again."

I feel a surge of emotion. He *was* a nice guy. And Leo knows it. He appreciates the niceness. This is something I've wanted him to see: the random people you meet in the woods. Confident. Crunchy. Eager to spend their free time frolicking in nature. I've never gone wrong with this particular tribe. The hikers. The skiers. The paddlers and mountaineers. There are a million ways to be outside, but this is the way I most love: motorless, physically active, a loving dance with the contours of the land. Mountain biking is one of those ways, and that nameless rider, who has just disappeared into the bushes, is one of those fellow spirits. And if Leo feels that same kinship, instinctively, without me saying a word, I can see the torch being passed.

"Okay!" Leo exclaims. "Let's go!"

Barreling!

The next two hours are an uphill battle. I manage to ride up the trail with surprising grace, sliding only a little on slick rocks. But Leo starts to resent the limits of his small bike. He dismounts and pushes; he rides a few level yards; then he dismounts and pushes again. Still, he never gives up. At seven, *I* would never have endured this kind of frustration. I would have become a sobbing, self-accusing mess. Leo keeps going. When we turn around, he goes slowly, negotiating the drops with care and precision. My daredevil son, who will happily climb onto any piece of furniture in our house and then jump onto any other piece of furniture, descends the hill with thoughtful caution.

"Am I barreling?" he asks.

"You're doing it just right."

And suddenly it dawns on me: This has all been *his* idea. I found the place, because I know how to use Google; but it was Leo who wanted to expand our two-wheeled horizons. I don't care that it's not really mountain biking, that we're hopelessly ill-equipped, that the trail barely rises above sea level. We're breaking new ground—literally. And I can see why people love it.

We go much farther than I expect, winding over slopes and crossing murky wetlands. It was still too early for mosquitoes, and we only had to cross one major puddle. I rushed straight through it, demonstrating to Leo how to properly muddy his tires.

"It's okay," I called. "Like, if you're gonna get dirty, this is the time to do it."

Just then, a trio of ATVs growled toward us. They steered clear, making sure not to splash us with the puddle water. "Nice day out!" they yelled over the rumbling of their quads.

Like clockwork, we reached the car just as Leo's blood sugar was audibly dropping. I packed up. We downed water and devoured rice cakes. Leo looked contemplatively through the window, at all the wall of trees we had just explored.

Then he bellowed, "Was that awesome, or was that awesome?"

And it was. For more reasons than he even knew.

WHEN YOU COME TO A FORK IN THE ROAD, TAKE IT

"You know, I could get into biking."

This is how my wife puts it, one summer morning, a few months into the COVID lockdown of 2020.

I nearly choke on my fruit smoothie.

"You... could?" I stammer.

She shrugs. "I mean—sure. I haven't really done it since I was a kid. That could be something to get into, right?"

I'm gobsmacked. After 15 years together, K. has never once expressed interest in two-wheeled conveyance of any kind. The idea has never seemed to cross her mind. We've ridden bicycles together exactly once. Yet somehow, on this bright June morning, riding around strikes her as a fine idea.

"Maybe you could see if there's a cheap used bike for sale?" she nudges.

"Yes," I say, ripping out my smartphone. "Absolutely. Already on it."

K. is a runner. That's always been her thing. She ran cross-country in high school. She started running again in her early twenties, and soon she finished her first marathon. She followed this up with several more marathons, until

38

running 26 miles became a totally feasible weekend option.

K's running is so inspiring that even I started running, something I had never once considered before we met. I ran several half-marathons, which deeply satisfied me. But K. was in a league of her own. She had a running group and top-notch footwear. She yearned to beat her best time, then beat it again. K. is a *real* runner, driven and passionate—whereas I just like to move around outside while I listen to audiobooks.

Times have changed. K. is busier now, thanks to the arrival of our young son and a fast-track career. Our old home in Pittsburgh was located a few blocks from Frick Park, one of the most dynamic urban green spaces in the country; our new home in Rhode Island is far more suburban. K. can't just bolt out the door and run for five uninterrupted miles through the woods.

What we have instead is a bike path, but even that isn't quick to reach on foot, and there are many stop signs and crosswalks between our front door and the trailhead. So for the first time in her adult life, my wife wants her own bike. She wants to regain the freedom of solo exercise, this time on two wheels.

Fake Exercise

I scour online classifieds, and I quickly find a decent model: a Fuji road bike, built for a petite woman, for $150. The seller informs me that the bike has barely been used. When I arrive at her house—heavily masked—I'm surprised how easily I can lift the bike onto my car rack. The featherweight frame had twenty-one gears and a pair of drop-bars. The model isn't fancy; Fujis are a brand you find in the sporting section at Walmart. But the bike is good as new, and it's designed to go *fast*.

K. likes the bike. We try a few family rides down the nearby path. The Fuji fits her perfectly, and we spend a few pleasant hours coasting under a summer sun.

But her interest quickly fades. One day she's riding; the next, she's not. K. only tries one ride by herself, and she doesn't like it. K. isn't an urban rider. She doesn't like navigating through motor traffic. She relies on sidewalks, which aren't purposed for bikes and make for rough riding. Even the path doesn't impress her; flat pavement is too easy to traverse, and she quickly gets bored.

"It just isn't really exercise," she declares. "You might as well be driving."

I disagree, but I saw her point. Rhode Island isn't a hilly state, and the rail-trails are level by design. K. isn't the type to stop and smell the flowers. She doesn't savor the scenery the way I do. Without a race to train for, her motivation fizzles. Within a fortnight, she has basically given up on cycling—certainly on her own.

I'm disappointed, but maybe not surprised. Once a runner, always a runner. Cycling is an acquired taste, and I doubt she'll ever have the patience to acquire it. So it goes.

Lemons Into Lemonade

One morning, I drive to Roger Williams Park, a sprawling Gilded Age green space on the edge of Providence. The sun is bright. A podcast is playing on our stereo. My son munches a banana in the backseat. In a few minutes, we'll park, unload our bikes, and pedal a quick three-miler around the pond.

CHA-CHUNK!

My Subaru rams a speed bump.

I've driven this route a hundred times, and I should know where the mounds of asphalt rise from the road. But I didn't notice it. Suddenly, I hear a grinding sound, coming from the rear of the car. I pull over, worried I've damaged my axle.

"What's that sound?" asks Leo.

"I'm not sure. Just wait here a sec."

I spring out of the car. I see the bike rack, which has collapsed. The metal framework clings to two nylon straps; the other straps and hooks have let go of the fissures in my car and sway uselessly. Our bikes dangle from the rack; they've dropped down to the level of the street. My son's bike is unharmed, but *my* bike has been dragged along the pavement. The tires look distorted, like they've been melted in a fire. The rims are bent beyond repair.

"Okay," I say, sliding into the driver's seat. "Looks like my bike is broken."

"We can't go biking?"

"We can't go biking, no. I have to get this home and see if I can fix it. Sorry I ruined our trip."

My son considers this unfortunate turn of events, the irreparable damage I've done, the abrupt change in plans.

He says, "Can I watch a movie?"

I can't fix the wheels, I know. No trueing machine on Earth can reshape those rims, and the timing is awful: in a few days, I'm planning to bike 140 miles across Connecticut. New wheels can be pricey; I could easily end up spending as much as the original cost of the whole bike. I fume over my stupidity. *How could I bumble over a speed bump like that? Why wasn't I paying closer attention? What was I thinking about, as I absentmindedly destroyed my most prized possession?*

Back home, I puzzle over what to do. I stand in my garage, staring at the mangled bike, hoping that if I linger here long enough, an answer will come to me. I scan the workbench, the Rubbermaid crates, and the yellow road bike in the corner. The one my wife has stopped using.

"Wait a minute," I say aloud.

I go to the Fuji, disconnect the wheels, and attach them to my own Trek hybrid. They lock into the frame, as if designed for my own bike. The tires are skinnier than I'm used to—I'll have to be careful riding over gravel and dirt—but they work perfectly well on pavement. The gearing is identical. Within five minutes, I've attached the chain, oiled the gears, and tested the new setup in our driveway.

The ride is smooth. They almost feel better than the originals.

I sheepishly confess all this to my wife. It's one thing to give a gift and learn that the recipient never uses it. It's another thing to manhandle that gift, rip it apart, and abandon its dissected corpse in your shed, all so you can go on vacation without spending extra money.

But K. isn't concerned. If she ever wants to bike again, we can invest in new rims. And to my surprise, she glances at my old rims—now bent, naked, and leaning against a cinder block wall.

"Maybe we could use those for decorations," she says. "Spray paint them? Hang them in the living room? That could look pretty cool, right?"

I marvel at this idea. I've seen this kind of decor in cycling-themed pubs and cafes across the country. It *could* be cool. And so fitting.

But we haven't yet. The rims remain in the corner of our garage, dusty and misshapen. Procrastination and lack of wall space may forever prevent us from hanging them.

Still, like so many things in life, it's a nice idea.

Keep Calm and Pedal On

I don't like the look of them. Two Guys, skulking down the bike path. I smell the cigarette smoke off their bodies, even though they're not smoking. They're older, maybe fifty, with greasy hair and sagging clothes. As I bike past them, I see the one guy's face—freshly cut in several places, a bandage pasted over his cheek. He looks like he's been in a fight.

"Afternoon," I say.

"Hey, there," they both answer, jutting their chins.

I wouldn't care. Their walk, their business, their lives. I'm on my bike, they're on foot, and they'll soon fade into the leafy background.

But I'm alone. My son was bringing up the rear, pedaling along on his miniature mountain bike. He just learned to balance a couple days ago, and he's still slow and unsteady.

"Beautiful day," I say.

"Yeah," the Two Guys grunt back, grinning cryptically.

We ride onward, and I'm relieved to leave the Two Guys behind. But Leo keeps stopping. He wants to rest. He takes in the scenery. He's never ridden so far on his own, and he's still adjusting to this particular exertion. This ride won't be long, and soon we'll turn around.

We pause at a park bench. We eat a couple of cereal bars, then swig from my water bottle. The Two Guys come closer. They're not walking fast, but their progress is steady. By the time I convince Leo to remount his bike, they're only a few paces away.

They murmur to each other. Visibly confidential. They're leering at us—or is that just my imagination?

Then I see the stick in the one guy's hand. The guy with the lacerated face. It's a hefty stick, waist-high. It would pass for a walking stick. But the difference between a walking stick and cudgel is what you decide to do with it.

The Two Guys approach. I tense, but I keep my face casual. Unconcerned. I glance at my son. I wondered who would hear me if I called for help. No one else occupies the bike path. But I see traces of houses through the foliage. If I'm struck, I just have to stay conscious, keep track of my phone, and I can shuffle us to safety. Attackers are always more jittery. There are two of them, yes, but if Leo runs, they might panic. Maybe I'll get hurt, but we'll survive. These guys will be taking a big risk. They'd be idiots to try to get away on foot.

"Hey," said the guy with the walking stick, "you know how far to Lang's Bowlarama?"

"Nah, sorry, man," I said in a fraternal tone. "I don't know it offhand."

The guy clucks his tongue. He looks sideways—a little shifty, but mostly frustrated. Just a guy with a cut-up face trying to get where he was going.

"Alright, thanks," he said.

And that's it.

They keep walking. We start to ride in the opposite direction. The distance between us widens, until they're only faraway specs.

I look at Leo, pedaling blissfully ahead of me, and a hundred emotions well up.

Stuff Happens

Two years ago, a woman was sexually assaulted in the nearby town of Coventry. The attacker grabbed her breast, then ran off. The police used surveillance video to track down a suspect, arrested him, and discovered a significant rap sheet.

The day we meet the Two Guys, my son and I are technically riding the same trail. When we first moved to the area, neighbors warned me about the path.

"It's a nice path," they said. "But keep a lookout. Stuff can happen."

I am a fanatical supporter of multi-use paths. I honestly believe that the rail-trail system is the most intelligent and impressive infrastructure developed in the past half-century. The national network of non-motorized paths has radically improved the quality of life in America, and in ways that can't be fully measured or described. I'm biased, of course, because I use these paths constantly; but I'm consistently awed by the achievements of the Rails-to-Trails Conservancy, which has overseen the construction of 24,600 miles of trails in the United States—roughly the circumference of the Earth. And as of this writing, 9,000 additional miles are currently planned.

But there is a dark side to the trails. Because it's true: *Stuff can happen.*

Stuff can happen anywhere, of course. In broad daylight. In your house. In a school or business. The single time I was mugged, it was on a suburban street in the middle of a sunny afternoon by a lone attacker with a claw hammer. And it wasn't just any street, but the street where I had recently bought a house. That was years ago, and I got away unharmed, but I'll never forget the terror of that moment. Such an assault felt so unlikely. Yet it happened.

Rail-trails have replaced defunct railroad lines, which often run through grim and lonesome landscapes. When you bike down these paths, you see the backs of warehouses, empty parking lots, walls of chain link fence, and the underbellies of bridges. Many of us ride rail-trails to get away from crowds; we seek out quiet and solitude, far from the moan of traffic.

On some paths, at certain times of year, I've biked for hours without passing a single other person. I love that kind of public privacy. But I always remind myself how vulnerable a solo cyclist is. The same isolation that makes trails so meditative can be dangerous, as the victim in Coventry learned only too well.

It's not just violence. People can get lost. People can forget to dress for the elements, or fail to drink enough water, or succumb to exhaustion. I once heard a story about a teenager with autism who wandered down a rail-trail and got lost for several days. Afraid and disoriented, he hid himself in the bushes, making himself difficult to find. Rail-trails are often classified as "linear parks," and like any park, you need to know your way around, even if "around" is a straight line.

On my own, I'm cavalier about trails. I've mended flat tires in the remotest forests of Western Pennsylvania, and I've laughed my way through lightning storms in the wilderness. I'm privileged in many ways—male, fit, youthful—and I routinely shrug off legitimate concerns.

With my son, the trail feels far less secure. If you ever want to destroy your faith in humanity, just become a parent; you will spend the rest of your life in a malaise of paranoia. The trail is still a peaceful escape, a monument to civic goodwill. But stuff happens. It always can.

All's Well That Ends Well

I stop my bike. Leo also stops. "Hey," I whisper. "I just have to say—those two guys back there?"

"The guys who asked for directions?"

"Yeah. I didn't like the look of them."

"You didn't like how they looked?"

"That's right. Maybe they were fine. They seemed nice enough. And nothing bad happened. That's the important thing. But I want you to know—I didn't trust them."

"You didn't trust them?"

"No. There was something about them. But *you* did everything right. And if something had happened—if they had tried to do something bad—I would have protected you, okay? And luckily, we didn't have to do anything, because it was just fine. Just—sometimes, you have to be careful. Because you don't know where people are coming from, or what they want."

Leo considers this. He leans into his handlebars. Then he nods. In that instant, I'm as grateful as I've ever been that he's healthy and happy and has never seen an act of violence in his life.

"Okay, Papa, can we keep biking now?"

"Sure," I say. "Let's keep biking."

Because we may not know what the next mile will bring. But that's not going to stop us.

We're Jammin'

Somewhere in the neighborhood of Olneyville, I trade small talk with a giant banana.

"I'm enjoying all the twenty-inch wheels on this ride," says the banana, laughing jovially.

I also laugh jovially. We both ride compact bikes with tiny wheels. His is a candy-colored fixie. Mine is a Dahon folding bike.

"I gotta say," I answer, "I love the costume."

"Thanks, man!" chortles the giant banana, and he pedals away, lost in a river of cyclists.

A banana outfit is hardly the goofiest thing I've seen tonight. I've pedaled alongside vampires, disco dancers, superheroes, and living skeletons. One burly guy is dressed as a Beanie Baby, another as a chicken. Beetlejuice and Jason Voorhees pop into my field of vision. One woman wears the regal dress and powdered wig of Marie Antoinette. A guy is wearing a giraffe costume so unwieldy I can't believe he's upright. Spokes and frames are dotted in Christmas lights; trailing behind are wings and veils and tresses. But the vast majority are zombies, pale, haggard, and spattered with blood. This *is* the Zombie Ride, after all. Undead is *in*.

And then there's me, dressed as—myself. Fall jacket, scarf, helmet, jeans. An ensemble so functional, I can't even pretend it's a costume. In the middle of a vast, mobile Halloween party, I'm the odd man out, the one who hasn't made any effort.

In my defense, I didn't know I could attend the PVD Bike Jam until a few hours before it started. Evenings are hard to predict in my household, especially on chilly Friday nights. I fully expected to read my son to sleep, then slump in front of Netflix for a few hours. But when I casually mentioned that the Bike Jam was happening tonight, my wife exclaimed, "Oh! *I* can put him to bed. You should go!"

K.'s enthusiasm was a pleasant surprise. Ever since COVID's Delta variant started spreading, we'd been conservative about our movements. But cycling is one social activity that feels low-risk. So I threw on some clothes, tossed my folding bike in the car, and drove to downtown Providence—completely forgetting that this was Halloween weekend.

At Burnside Park, in the middle of downtown Providence, I pushed my bike into a festive crowd of two hundred cyclists, every one of them in costume.

Understand, I am *not* a wallflower. I love to interact with people, especially people I don't know.

But here, I'm slow to acclimate. This is my first PVD Bike Jam. I don't know anyone, and none of my cyclist friends could join me on such short notice. With so much social distancing, I've basically forgotten how to talk with people. I'm alone, tired from the week, and couldn't be bothered to dress up. Like, *what a dud.*

And although the PVD Bike Jam is open to anyone and prides itself on diversity and access, I'm clearly one of the oldest people here. I just celebrated a lackluster forty-second birthday, and in this crowd of bohemian twenty-somethings, I feel ancient. Most of these people seem to know each other, and they talk excitedly in tight-knit bunches. Add to this my odd-looking bike—a trifold eight-speed with sixteen-inch wheels—and I can't help but feel self-conscious.

But I stifle my misgivings. I've finally made it. I'm *here*. This is my tribe, whether they know it or not. Once the music starts blasting, and throngs of cyclists roll into collective motion, I assure myself I'm in the right place. I merge with traffic, flanked on all sides by imaginary beasts and flesh-eaters, and the memories come rushing back.

Roll Out

My first social bike ride didn't take place in Providence, or even the United States, but in Costa Rica, where I lived for two years.

I was new in San José, the nation's grim capital, and I didn't really know anyone. In the first few weeks, I fell in with a bike activist group called the "Chepecletas." One night, I spent a few blissful hours pedaling back-streets with a hundred-or-so Costa Rican cyclists. I became friendly with the lead organizer, Roberto Gúzman, and wrote about the Chepecletas for a local newspaper, where I'd started working as a staff reporter.

Throughout my expat experience, I biked regularly, exploring the twisted lanes of San José. The Chepecletas helped me adjust to Central American traffic and introduced me to some of my first friends. Urban cycling isn't exactly popular in Costa Rica, and I doubt I would have felt so brave without them.

Next, I moved to Phoenix, Arizona. Again, I knew no one and had no idea how the city ticked. A few weeks in, I learned about the Car Resistance Action Party, or CRAP, and joined them for a ride on a blistering summer solstice. There I met Alex Steiner, the CRAP ride's impossibly charismatic organizer, and wrote another article for another local paper.

Bicycle clubs are as old as the bike itself, and the popularity of group rides was a driving force for first paving American roads. In recent decades, social rides are synonymous with bicycle advocacy; movements like Critical Mass were designed to assert the rights of cyclists, no matter how many motorists flipped them off.

Today, group rides are commonplace in American cities, but they often retain their counter-cultural roots: riders haul speaker systems on cargo bikes and blast dance music into the night air; the massive congregations are a chance to flaunt urban fashions, show off customized machines, and celebrate with craft beer. At a glance, riders are a rainbow of social classes and gender identities. You could call a group ride a "demonstration," in every sense of the word.

The ride itself is a magical blend—communal, aerobic, zero-emission, and basically free. As I roll out of Burnside Park, surrounded by so many strangers, I wonder how I've managed to exist without this for so long.

An Unexpected Party

A few miles into the route, the leader turns his bike into a city park. Riders trickle past playground equipment and chain link fence, and they pool around a well-lit basketball court. Bikes are laid in the grass, and the crowd morphs into a massive dance party.

This, I wasn't expecting. I didn't realize there would be a "party stop"—much less *two* party stops—and it's one of the many Bike Jam rituals you just have to experience to understand. Costumed riders bop and gyrate, their silhouettes sharp against the light of streetlamps. Much of the park is lost in darkness, and the whole scene feels joyful and rebellious.

I don't dance much, so I stick to the sidelines, reminding myself how much I'll love this next time, when I can convince a friend or two to come along. For now, I take it all in, the tapestry of conversations, the BMX guys doing tricks on the blacktop, the ever-growing circle of dancers. Remixes of "Thriller" and "Time Warp" throb from speakers, and even the lawn seems to vibrate beneath my soles.

A half-hour later, the ride starts again. The crowd pours into the street and flows through neighborhoods. The queue is long; our numbers stretch for blocks and blocks. At each traffic light, the leaders pause for two full cycles so the group can stay together. Cars pause, waiting for the parade to pass. Some drivers seem to grumble behind their windshields, but far more honk their horns in encouraging little bursts. Naturally, the exuberant riders cheer and whistle in reply.

One graying man—much closer to my age—asks about my folding bike. "How is it?" he asks, "Other than being able to fit in your pocket?"

I'm so delighted to talk with someone, I pummel the guy with questions. I learn that he grew up in Olneyville; he's an electrical engineer; he travels a great deal for work; and he recently moved back from Florida, where he had a regular group ride and was spoiled by the level streets. The highest point in their neighborhood was apparently thirty feet above sea level. I talk with his wife about her visit to Amsterdam. This conversation leads to others, and soon I'm jabbering with everyone I see. *This* is what I love—riding and schmoozing, like a mixer on wheels.

Somewhere in the West End, a guy steps out of his apartment building and calls out, "*What are you raising awareness for?*"

Riders just stare at him, unsure how to answer. In an instant, this guy will vanish, left to wonder who the hell we were. Finally, someone calls back, "Just riding a bike!"

"I should come along!" the guy rejoins.

"Do it!" someone exclaims. But it's not *someone*. I'm the one exclaiming.

As the blocks whisk past, I feel what I wanted to feel: the surge of endorphins, the revival of my mojo. My fatigue fades away. With each mile, excitement builds. Chatter gets louder, wheels accelerate. We power up hills and coast around corners, weaving and mingling. I look back and see the dark mass of humanity stretched a mile behind me. I smile at our galaxy of safety lights.

We ride past the Providence Public Library, which is apparently hosting a wedding. Men in tuxedos cheer us on, waving as we pass. We course through Downcity, where we blend with the regular weekend nightlife. We cross a bridge and watch city lights glisten in the Providence River.

And even though it's 11 p.m., and I have a long day tomorrow, and I still have to pack up my kit and drive home, I wish this night would go on and on. I could ride another ten miles with this legion of strangers and still feel the thrill of their company.

But I can also wait. Because I'll be back. I've broken myself in. And in just a few weeks, the cycle will begin anew.

Part 2:
Oh, Pioneers!

THE WORLD ACCORDING
TO THOMAS STEVENS

"I am bowling along beneath overhanging peach and mulberry trees, following a volunteer horseman to Mohammed Ali Khan's garden. Before reaching the garden a gang of bare-legged laborers engaged in patching up a mud wall favor me with a fusillade of stones, one of which caresses my ankle, and makes me limp like a Greenwich pensioner when I dismount a minute or two afterward..."
—Thomas Stevens
Around the World on a Bicycle

LIKE MANY TRAVEL writers, Thomas Stevens wrote in the first person. He also wrote in the present tense, so everything he recounts feels immediate, as if his journey is unfolding in real time. Over the course of many hundreds of pages, the reader travels with Stevens, eats with Stevens, weathers rainstorms with Stevens. When Stevens outwits thieves in Persia, we're right there with him. When he listens to "Hungarian

Gypsy music" in Serbia, we hear it, too. When he narrowly evades a herd of stampeding mustangs in the American frontier, we also duck and cover. With every crank of his pedal, we ride alongside, absorbing the same sensations.

But there's one thing missing from *Around the World on a Bicycle*, Stevens' mammoth memoir from 1887: the author himself.

Nowhere in his two volumes and forty-one chapters does Stevens bother to explain *why* he decided to ride a penny-farthing across three continents. He never once mentions his parents, his childhood, or a prior career. Even his titular bicycle, which carries him 13,500 miles over mountains and deserts, has no origin story; it simply appears out of the ether. The first chapter opens with a flowery description of his ride away from San Francisco and through the surrounding hills. You might expect some kind of flashback, but no; Stevens has hit the road, and he'll continue hitting it for two years straight.

Understand, though: Stevens isn't shy about his own opinion. He assesses the attractiveness of every woman he meets. He analyzes every meal and guesthouse in microscopic detail. He recounts whole histories and cultural traditions to the best of his ability, and then decides how they measure up to the standards of Western Civilization. Because he's riding a bicycle, Stevens is particularly preoccupied with road conditions, and he casually judges entire regions by their traversability. Stevens has unwavering confidence in his own perspective, and he assumes that we do, too—even if we have no idea who he is.

From a literary perspective, *Around the World on a Bicycle* is missing vital context. Take a similar book, like Cheryl Strayed's *Wild*, and you'll find a memoir of loss and addiction that also happens to take place on the Pacific Crest Trail. The most respected travelogues are usually couched in introspection. *Lands of Lost Borders*, by Kate Harris, is also about a cyclist riding thousands of miles across Asia, but in order to explain the importance of her journey, Harris chronicles much of her life up to that point. In contrast, Stevens unburdens himself of any past or motivation. There's nothing to him. He could be any able-bodied Victorian male with a taste for adventure.

The most revealing passage isn't in the story itself, but in the front matter:

To
Colonel Albert A. Pope,
of Boston, Massachusetts,
whose liberal spirit of enterprise, and generous confidence
in the integrity and
ability of the author, made the tour
Around the World on a Bicycle
possible, by unstinted financial patronage, is this volume
respectfully dedicated

There you have it: a young man writes his first book, and he dedicates it to his bankroller. Granted, Col. Pope was a prominent bicycle manufacturer at the time. Stevens owned a bicycle—one he'd bought with his own money for an 1884 trip across the United States—but Pope gifted him a nickel-plated Columbia Express and contracted him to write about his two-wheeled travels for *Outing*, a magazine Pope owned. Stevens would later draw on those articles to form *Around the World on a Bicycle*. How all this came to pass, though, would be anybody's guess, because the book never mentions these arrangements—nor Pope, nor anyone Stevens knows or cares about—again.

But *Around the World on a Bicycle* isn't literature, nor does it have any ambitions to be. Stevens may be the first human to circle the globe on a bicycle, and he may have chronicled the minutiae of that saga, but Stevens' book and Strayed's *Wild* don't stem from the same tradition. *Wild* is travel writing. *Around the World on a Bicycle* is something else entirely: it's sports porn.

Outdoor Fetish

Let's get one thing out of the way: I *love* sports porn.

While I'm sure there is "sports porn" intended for genuine sexual gratification, I of course mean something more colloquial: texts and images that excite consumers on a primal level. This more wholesome brand of sports porn celebrates athletic achievement in all its visual glory, perhaps motivating the consumer to attempt similar feats, but offers little narrative substance. Like actual pornography, sports porn doesn't tell a story so much as serve up an exciting scenario: What if you biked down a mountainous Chilean barrio? What if you went fly fishing in the remotest rivers of Siberia? Or in this case, what if you rode your high-wheeled bicycle all the way around the planet?

Specifically, I love outdoors porn—and bicycle porn in particular. As an avid rider who writes regularly about cycling, I could watch vloggers pedal over the Rockies all day. I devour whole issues of *Adventure Cyclist*, the official magazine of the Adventure Cycling Association, and every last field report. I attended the Banff Mountain Film Festival several years in a row, where I watched film after film of adrenaline junkies BASE jumping off cliffs or paddling kayaks over waterfalls.

Video is now the dominant medium for sports porn, which makes perfect sense, because moving pictures require little explanation and can literally zoom in on physical action. This is the kind of high-octane excitement that GoPro cameras were designed for. Today, it's easy for weekend warriors to shoot at high frame-rates and incorporate slo-mo and speed-ramps into their videos; even amateur productions can look spectacular. More and more often, solo sportsmen can make masterpieces on their own: gravel bikers journey into the Kyrgyzstani wilderness with their prosumer drones, and they return as YouTube influencers with thousands, or even millions, of followers. Any attempt at real plot would ruin the mojo.

But before video, there were glossy magazines like *Outside*, *Backpacker*, and *Dirt Rag*, periodicals that are often described in the journalism industry as "aspirational." I cite these titles lovingly: they are the few glossies I've ever actually subscribed to or read cover-to-cover. I have spent much of my own career writing aspirational articles, like how to ride a bike in Taiwan or where to grab brunch in Providence. But while magazines like *Outside* publish in-depth profiles about serious topics, their appeal for many is largely pictorial. Like *National Geographic*'s stunning landscape panoramas and aerial shots, sports porn photos of Himalayan ice-climbers and trail-running through Scotland will knock the wind out of you. The next thing you know, you've ordered $300 worth of gear from REI and hired a personal trainer.

Before moving pictures existed, though, Thomas Stevens was stirring imaginations with his words, and sports porn is the genre he helped create. In 1886, the high-wheel bicycle (known by many as an Ordinary or a penny-farthing, a reference to the large and small British coins its wheels resembled) was roughly equivalent to the iPhone in 2022: a relatively new technology that had completely transformed modern society. Europeans and Americans were still grasping the possibilities of this magical new machine, and Stevens seized the moment; he vowed to ride across the United States, England, Europe, the Middle East, and Asia, completing his journey in Yokohama, Japan. The route was arbitrary, as all round-the-world tours are, but Stevens is still the first known cyclist to satisfy the public with this claim. Stevens pedaled through countries he knew his readers would never visit, and he vividly described the people he met. In the same spirit as any pornographic text, readers were invited to switch out the actual narrator for their own globetrotting fantasy. Nobody cared *who* Thomas Stevens was. What they wanted to know was how he did it and what it was like when he got there.

The Man in Full

To be fair, I didn't "read" *Around the World on a Bicycle* so much as listen to it. Vintage copies on eBay can cost hundreds of dollars, and I struggled to find an unabridged reprint. An inexpensive ebook version was easy to find, but I was reluctant to read 1,000 pages of purple prose on a backlit screen. Instead, I found a recording produced by LibriVox—a free archive of public domain writings that functions like a Project Gutenberg of audiobooks—and I dedicated several weeks to Stevens' book, which is read in tandem by several volunteer narrators.

Day after day, I played Stevens' book on my car stereo. On the bike trail, earbud affixed, I gorged on chapters. The book echoed in my kitchen as I cooked or washed dishes, much to my family's chagrin. Travelogues are a double whammy for the reader, because the geographic journey mirrors the progression of sentences. The bike wheel turns slowly uphill; the paper page turns in the reader's fingers; the MP3's time-stamp ticks along, second by second.

As that journey continued, I found myself torn. On the one hand, I liked Stevens and could only imagine what a pleasure it was to know him. He's eloquent, dashing, and good-humored. The way he describes himself, Stevens seems gracious to friends and brass-knuckled to antagonists. He is genuinely curious about everything he sees, from folk dances in Eastern Europe to dining etiquette in Kurdistan. Stevens takes pains to learn local languages, to make friends wherever he goes. He compliments and admires much of what he sees: His awestruck description of the Taj Mahal is tear-jerkingly sincere.

Like all great travelers, he takes everything in stride; when Stevens is arrested in Afghanistan and escorted back to Persia, he expresses little more than disappointment. "As the golden dome of Imam Riza's sanctuary glimmers upon my retreating figure yet a fourth time as I reach the summit of the hill whence we first beheld it," he writes, "I breathe a silent hope that I may never set eyes on it again." If there's anything a cross-country cyclist loathes, it's backtracking.

Yet Stevens was a product of his era: he places absolute faith in his Anglo-Saxon virtues, and he finds novel ways to trivialize every other ethnicity. He has no problem describing people as "savages" and comparing their behaviors to children or even animals. In one passage, Stevens is forcibly escorted by a dark-skinned soldier in the Pashtun hills, and his description of the man amounts to straight-up minstrelsy. He also carries a revolver, which was common at the time, but he brags about using random wildlife for target practice. From a modern viewpoint, Stevens' boorish attitudes remain unsettling to the very last page.

Sports porn still struggles with this archetype—the brave white male seeking glory in exotic lands. In fairness, I have seen the genre diversify in recent years, largely thanks to social media, but the go-to lead character is still a scruffy blonde guy with a California cadence. Outdoorsy Americans tend to have conspicuous freedom and safety nets that make their lifestyles possible. Nowhere is this privilege more evident than in their rationales, often spoken in voiceover: "I didn't want to spend my life stuck in an office," or, "I needed to push myself to try something new"—the usual declarations of young men with a granola streak and nothing more pressing to worry about.

I can't criticize them too much, because I am part of that tribe—an obsessive cross-country cyclist who spends much of his free time reading about far-flung expeditions by bike. As a scruffy white guy, I could step into any of those YouTube fantasias and no one would notice. Almost 90 years after Stevens' death, I remain his target readership. And although the penny-farthing was soon replaced with the "safety bicycle," Stevens and I use roughly the same vehicle for roughly the same purpose: to explore, to challenge ourselves, to connect with the world.

Back to the Source

In the Ocean State Libraries system, I can't find a single edition of *Around the World on a Bicycle*, in print or digital versions. Instead, I track down a copy at the Providence Athenaeum, a library so historic that it used to loan books to Edgar Allan Poe.

But this isn't just any copy. The Athenaeum has an *original* printing of Stevens' book, released in two volumes in 1887 and 1888. What's more, handwritten notations in each book verify that the volumes were acquired in July and September of their respective publication years. These copies, now tattered from over a century of use, their spines chipped and cracked, were hot off the presses when they joined the Athenaeum's collection.

One of the librarians carefully sets up the books on a table, to make sure I don't strain the covers. She's never heard of Thomas Stevens, and when she sees a picture of the author in the opening pages, she guesses he's riding a unicycle. She sits at the desk behind me while I read, a gesture I appreciate. Seeing the book firsthand is a euphoric moment, and I'm grateful for someone to witness it.

What I didn't realize was that Stevens' book is illustrated; between them, the volumes contained 180 black-and-white plates. The etchings are artful and detailed; I could frame any one of them and proudly hang it in my home. As a drawn character, Stevens appears again and again, riding his bicycle or standing beside it. He finds himself in wildly mixed company, fashions changing all around him, from top hats to fezes to turbans to jingasa. It's hard to tell how much the artist embellished, of course. Stevens carried a camera, and he mentions snapping pictures, but he also rode alone, and there was no Google Images search to verify his accounts.

As critical as I am of Victorian culture, I can't help but fall under Stevens' spell. I've already devoured the audiobook, yet I still have plenty of room for dessert. Sports porn is most effective when it's audacious: people aren't *supposed* to have fun in such dangerous ways, yet here they are, free-climbing up sheer sandstone. Stevens didn't reveal much about himself, but he loved being the center of attention. The front wheel of his penny-farthing was fifty inches tall, and Stevens coasted into villages where bicycles had never been seen. In his telling, Stevens constantly explains what the bicycle is, and he entertains crowds by demonstrating its use. More than once, strangers offer to buy the bike from him. He craved the attention, and readers were eager to pay it.

For a 21st-century reader like me, the real value of *Around the World on a Bicycle* is accidental: It freezes time. Stevens was a sportsman and tourist; he saw the world at street level. He may not have been a reliable anthropologist, but the author painstakingly described what these lands looked and felt like to an ordinary Western visitor. Stevens exhibits a mindfulness that modern people still labor to attain. Given enough time, pornography transforms into documentary. To Stevens, writing a book about a global cycling tour was a business op with a built-in publicity stunt. Today, his account sheds light on a bygone world.

And the inspiration remains—timeless and pure, unsullied by subtext or character development. More than a century later, Stevens still urges readers on, to propel ourselves forward, to see how far we can go.

Re[inforc]ing the Wheel

I HAVE REACHED my breaking point. And so has my rear tire.

Today is Saturday. A midsummer morning. The bike path is shady and cool. Sunbeams shoot through the foliage. I coast into forest and over bridges, a giddy grin on my face. All week, I've looked forward to this one free morning, my single chance to get out and ride.

Then I hear it—the burst of air. A long wheeze follows as my inner tube flattens beneath me. In a few seconds, my rear wheel is shot, and I'm stuck pushing the bike into a little gazebo.

By coincidence, the gazebo marks a trailhead, and another cyclist is resting on a nearby bench. He's an older guy with a mustache. I ask him for a pump, and he eagerly retrieves it. I carry my own, but the pump is small and the pressure low. My tubes are self-sealing, I explain, so if I can pump enough air into the tube, the tire should fix itself.

Why should this work? Because I specially ordered a "slime" tube. The rubber is laced with green liquid. I've never used a "slime" tube before, but my last mechanic fervently recommended them. In theory, the "slime" is supposed to congeal over the puncture. The mechanic was so confident, I didn't even bring a patch kit.

But the tire doesn't inflate. As I lean into the pump's handle, desperately shoving oxygen into the tube, little green bubbles pop around the valve. The wheel flattens again and again. I hand back the pump, thanking the man profusely. I also swallow my rage; this is my dozenth flat in a single summer. Not just on this bike, but on *both* my bikes. Somehow, I just can't keep the wheels buoyant. And now I'm alone, ten miles from home, in a parking lot in rural Rhode Island.

I lock up the bike. I call an Uber. For a half-hour, the driver meanders the country roads of Coventry and Warwick. She tells me tales about her career as a lunch lady at a local school, but I barely listen. I'm livid. I've squandered my one free morning. Now I'll go home, to pick up my car, attach the bike rack, and drive thirty minutes back to that same parking lot. For one hour of riding, I will waste 90 minutes in cars.

I will never let this happen again, I think. *Fuck flats.*

Lifting the Curse

If anything makes me superstitious, it's flat tires. In a good season, I can ride hundreds of miles without a scratch. Maybe I hit a thorn, but a single patch does the trick. I continue to ride, using that one little bandaid for another hundred miles, hopefully more.

In a *bad* season, my inner tube fizzles over and over, and for no discernible reason. One spring, back in Phoenix, I endured eight flats in a row. I used patches. I switched tubes. I checked the tires for stray debris. I checked for holes and wear. I checked the rims, in case a spoke had jutted through. Still, the flats kept coming, sometimes within sight of my garage. I couldn't understand it. One bike was practically new. The other had always been dependable. What was I doing wrong?

Friends speculated, but no two theories were alike. They told me about the desert, how the radical shifts in temperature affect the air pressure inside the tire; when a tube suddenly sags, you get pinch flats. That sounded reasonable, but why hadn't it happened the year before?

Other friends talked about the cacti, how microscopic spines are carried in the wind and embed themselves in rubber. That also sounded scientific enough, but how could any bicycle function, if they were just pincushions for invisible thorns?

After a while, I start to blame myself. I think: *Maybe I deserve to have flat tires. Maybe I'm not supposed to ride a bicycle.*

I'm not a superstitious person by nature. I don't throw salt over my shoulder or start hyperventilating around black cats. But I do have a karmic streak. A rash of bad luck—even a first-world problem like repeated flat tires—gets me looking up at the sky and wondering what I did wrong. As this spring becomes a minefield of deflation, I wonder what sin I've committed.

But I've had enough. I *don't* deserve flats. I've done everything right. I've tried new tires, new rims, and a pile of new tubes. I've carefully monitored my PSI. I've tried Presta and Shrader valves, brand-name and generic. I've fixed the punctures myself, and I've consulted professionals. Every few days, no matter which bike I ride, my tires burst open. One patch is followed by another. Nothing works. It's the definition of insanity.

So I break the cycle—so to speak. If I can't trust a tube, then I wouldn't *use* a tube. I'll find a different kind of tire. Tubeless. Airless. Totally solid.

I learn about airless tires by accident. I'm doing some virtual window-shopping when I stumble into the website for Citizen Bike. Citizen is based in the U.S., and they specialize in nice-but-inexpensive folding bikes. Citizen makes it very easy on the buyer; you pick your model and color, and then you can add extras to your delivery. After all, they're sending you a box with a bike in it; why not add some other doodads to fill the extra space?

Do you want a comfy seat? A luggage rack? A tote bag? A multitool? An indoor trainer? How about airless tires?

I squint. *What the hell are airless tires?*

"Want to ride flat-free forever?" the website reads. "Upgrade to a set of airless Muffin tires for $119. These tires can ride from MIAMI to TOKYO without a pit-stop."

Flat-free? Forever? Is that even possible?

I try to imagine what that would be like—a world without flat tires. Could I ride over hidden nails, jagged gravel, shattered bottles, without fear? Could I jump curbs without popping? Could I really leave the patch kit at home, along with my levers, hand-pump, and glue? How much time would that save, if I never had to huddle in a ditch and perform invasive surgery on a yard of floppy latex? How many grease stains would I never have to scrub off my fingers? How many spares would I never have to carry?

All this sounds too good to be true. If omnipotent tires

exist, why doesn't everybody have them? Still, I have to try them myself.

"Say, do you sell airless tires?" I ask the clerk at my local bike shop.

The clerk frowns. "Do you mean airless, or tubeless?"

I hesitate. I have no idea what the difference is.

"So, tubeless tires need a special wheel," he explains. "You still have to pump them up, but they don't, like, have a separate tube. An airless tire..." He shrugs. "So, I've heard of those, but we don't install them here. Maybe at the other store. But I heard they're super hard to put on. And frankly? I'm worried we'd damage our tools."

I thank him, but I don't like what I was hearing. I easily found airless tires on the Internet. I could order them that very moment. But what then? Are they really so hard to install that a professional bike mechanic will refuse to even try? If a pro can't handle it, what chance do I have?

The bottom line is this: airless tires are new. The concept is nearly as old as the bicycle, but the nice thing about regular tires is that they're light; most of their volume is—literally—air.

Until recently, an airless tire has just been a circle made of solid rubber. It's heavy and dense. There isn't much give. For a hybrid bike like mine, a rigid tire makes for rocky riding. There's a reason early bikes were called "bone shakers."

But the technology is changing, fast. One pioneer is Tannus, a manufacturer based in South Korea. Instead of a curved rubber block, Tannus has patented a "multi-cell foam tire." It's tough but light, and you can install Tannus tires on your regular rims; the company even sends you a special tool. The material is pliable; it mimics different levels of air pressure. The tires are guaranteed to be puncture-proof for 5,000 miles—which is twice the distance I've ridden in the past three years.

I like the sound of that. But a pair of Tannus tires, sized for a 700c hybrid, cost about $150. That's nothing to sneeze at. And what if I fail to install them? What if I'm not handy enough—or even physically strong enough—to stretch them over the metal rims? Clearly, Tannus tires are too new to interest a real mechanic. I might save years' worth of patches and headaches; but I might also throw away $150 and still have no permanent solution.

So I do what anyone would do: I go to YouTube.

The de facto expert on airless tires is a guy named Cruise. He describes himself as "an American cyclist living [in] Japan with my Vietnamese wife, Thuong." Cruise is fit, cheerful, and blond, and he hosts his videos in an accent so friendly he almost sounds Canadian. For a quarter of an hour, he walks you through every detail of the Tannus experience—and with help from his wife, Cruise installs an airless tire in real time, narrating as he goes.

Without Cruise's guidance, I might've chickened out. But it's reassuring to see a fairly ordinary person put the wheel together. Cruise doesn't hide the fact that this is a difficult technique to master, and I might require a second person to help. But just to see it done—that is motivation enough.

I order the Tannus tires. And pray—in my quasi-superstitious way—that I'm making the right decision.

Rubber to the Road

The tires arrive a few days later. They are ostentatiously packaged in transparent plastic boxes, many times larger than the tires themselves. Like a lot of technical toys in the 21st Century, the package includes barebones paper instructions—and a YouTube link.

I remove the old tires without a second thought, but the rim tape gives me pause. Tannus instructs new users to rip away that narrow strip in the groove of my wheel. I've never done this before; I've never even thought about rim tape. This step always feels like The Point of No Return—when you start undoing parts you have no idea how to put back together.

The secret to Tannus tires is the "locking pin." These "pins" are tiny plastic rectangles, only a few millimeters across; if you dropped one in a mound of Legos, you might never find it again. But they're tough little widgets; my task is to insert them into holes in the tire. In a few minutes, they stud the circumference, like colored rivets.

Next step: to pull the tire over the rims.

This is the hardest part, and many a blogger has confessed to giving up. For this reason alone, Tannus novices will head to a bike shop and surrender to a professional. I would gladly do so myself. But I know what I've signed up for; either I'll get the tires on, or nobody will.

Fastening the tires is every bit as hard as they said it would be. I yank. I stretch. I push and pull until my fingers scream for mercy. I do all this on my back porch, under a withering sun. Sweat drips off my nose. I grunt and curse, because the tire just won't fall into place. One side looks secure, but then it flops away, and I have to start all over.

On the other hand, I *do* succeed.

I coax the tire onto the rims, and I jam the locking pins into the metal groove. One by one, the pins relent with a satisfying click. This is the strangest part of the process, because I'm not sure what the end result should look like. The diagram is vague. Cruise's YouTube video never zooms in on his handiwork. I can't consult anyone, because no one I know could answer the simple question, "Does this look right?"

After an hour of mashing and molding, massaging and manipulating, both tires are attached. To the naked eye, they look like regular bike tires, the kind you would find on any Trek hybrid. I push the bike through our gate and onto our suburban street. I pedal, and the wheels turn over tarmac.

They *do* feel different. Many bloggers warn about this. They drag a little, as if I were riding over glue. But I can live with that. I bounce over cracks and potholes. I bump the edge of a manhole cover. The Tannus tires are stiff, true, but I don't mind that, either.

Because they will last. They'll withstand almost anything. And I have 5,000 miles to get used to them. That kind of freedom—it just about leaves me breathless.

Behold, the Kwiggle

When I first see a picture of the Kwiggle, I can't figure out what I'm looking at. It doesn't look like a bicycle. Yes, there are two wheels. Yes, there are pedals. But I can't find the seat. The Kwiggle's shape vaguely reminds me of a C-clamp, the kind used for carpentry.

But then I see the Kwiggle on YouTube. Commercials. Unboxings. People riding it. And everything changes.

The Kwiggle has twelve-inch wheels, about the circumference of a dinner plate. The downtube is so low that it seems to skirt the ground. Instead of a seat post, it has an arm that bends away from the handlebars, like a robot that's flexing its bicep. The seat is tiny, and it hovers over the rest of the machine. The bike looks impossible to ride—at first.

But then I watch people do it. They mount the bike in one fluid motion. Their posture is perfectly straight. Instead of bending over, the cyclist basically stands up. Kwiggle riders look like they're levitating through the air, steadied by a tiny handlebar.

The Kwiggle is eye-catching on the road, yet there's a

more practical reason I stumble into it on the Internet: I'm on the lookout for a folding bike—something I can use for commutes, maybe even touring, that I can store easily.

And this is the Kwiggle's *pièce de resistance*: the frame collapses into itself; the folded dimensions are about twenty-two inches by fifteen inches by ten inches. You could theoretically slip a folded Kwiggle into a large bookbag.

And it's purportedly the most compact folding bicycle ever made.

But where did it come from? What mad genius invented such a strange-looking device? And where could I find one?

The answers:

Hanover, Germany.

Karsten Bettin.

Nowhere in the Western Hemisphere. *Yet.*

Upright Citizen

Some years ago, Karsten Bettin was watching the Tour de France on television. As two lead riders pumped their way up a hill, they stood up. This is a routine tactic among racers; they use their full weight to add power to the rotation of their pedals.

But one rider struggled to stand. He kept sitting back down on his saddle. He went back and forth like this, standing and sitting, in a torturous effort to out-muscle his opponent.

"I thought, 'Why is it so hard for him to ride standing up for longer?'" Bettin tells me. "Surely he has eight hours every day to practice this crucial skill."

Bettin is a mechanical engineer, and he's also a lifelong cyclist, so the problem intrigued him. He wondered: Could he condition himself to stand up on his bicycle? Could he ride exclusively in an upright position, without ever sitting down? And if it were possible, could this have a positive impact on his ride?

"From that day on, I only rode my bike standing up to find out if it was trainable," Bettin says. "And indeed, it got better and better. But it was more strenuous. So I thought about whether and how it might be possible to make riding—while standing—more comfortable."

And from that one question, the Kwiggle was born.

Inside the Fold

Here is what I like about the Kwiggle: you can ride it almost anywhere, but you can also make it disappear.

Folding bikes have become extremely popular in recent years. As more people commute by bicycle, especially in dense cities, the demand for folders has exploded.

The trendiest example is Brompton, a manufacturer based in London. Brompton bicycles has a patented tri-fold design; the frame folds so small, it can reportedly fit into an airplane's overhead compartment. Bromptons aren't cheap, but they've become a hot commodity. When I recently inquired about buying a Brompton at my local bike shop, I was told there was a wait of at least eight weeks.

But a compact folding bike comes at a cost. Quality models are expensive, easily a thousand dollars or more. The wheels are usually smaller, which means you're more likely to "feel the road." The mechanics are simplified, so you rarely have more than a few gears; indeed, Brompton's biggest seller is a single-speed.

And there's one drawback that remains unspoken: a folded bike still takes up space. Most bikes fold in the middle, so it only cuts its size in half. You can often remove the seat or fold down the handlebars, release the pedals or flip them upward; but the wheels keep their full diameter. Cheaper models are notoriously heavy; yes, you can fit it in the trunk of your car, but you may slip a disk trying to lift it.

Then there's the airport. Even Bromptons may raise eyebrows at security checkpoints. Entire YouTube tutorials are dedicated to convincing airport staff to allow your Brompton onboard, because so few TSA agents are familiar with the brand. Meanwhile, good luck trying to carry your folding bike onto a city bus, or even a subway during peak hours. Folding bikes are versatile and liberating, but they're still a lot like regular bikes. And if there's anything the modern world doesn't want to deal with, it's bicycles.

The Kwiggle is different. It's tiny. It doesn't *look* like a bike, especially when folded. You really *can* stuff it into regular luggage. It only weighs 20 lbs., so it's easy to carry. Every extraneous inch has been removed, leaving only the most definitive components. Yet it still *is* a bicycle. The Kwiggle isn't just a glorified scooter. It has three gears. The wheels are durable. And it moves.

All this is exciting for a folding bike. The design is everything you want from German engineering, including corrosion-resistant rims and sprockets that somehow work with only eight-to-ten teeth. Bettin did cite this as a motivation; he noticed that some countries, like China, are pro-cycling but have limited space for parking, so bikes end up in tangled piles on the street. The Kwiggle can be discreetly carried into your office or factory, and no one is the wiser.

And yet—a small folding bike isn't what Bettin intended. There are a few ultra-small folding bikes already on the market, most notably the A-Bike, which purports to be the smallest *and* lightest model. The fact that Kwiggle even folds seems more like a side-effect than a primary goal.

"If I had intended to invent the world's smallest folding bike, I certainly wouldn't have come up with this solution," Bettin tells me. "Originally, I wanted to build a bicycle that could be ridden comfortably—while standing up."

A Kwiggle Bit of This, a Kwiggle Bit of That

Bettin tinkered with his design for years. He often took apart children's bikes in order to build his prototypes. Bettin had a regular job as an engineer, so he would devote his nights to the Kwiggle. Once he finished a version, he would test-ride it around the neighborhood.

"And the more mature the prototypes became, the more fun it was," he tells me in an email. "After each trip, I came to the same conclusion: great riding is worth all this effort. There is rarely another device in the world that offers so much fun with this simultaneously physiologically optimal movement."

Part of that "physiologically optimal movement" is the crooked seat-post. Unlike a regular bike, the Kwiggle's post actually *swivels back and forth.* This helps the rider's upright pose; instead of riders moving their hips to accommodate the pedals, the frame moves to accommodate riders' hips. This innovation is the origin of the Kwiggle's name: "wiggle" for the movement, and "K" for Karsten, the inventor's first name.

This is arguably Bettin's most important breakthrough, far more impressive than the Kwiggle's other attributes, but it's also the least obvious. If you're passing a Kwiggle rider, you probably won't notice that "wiggle" motion.

Karsten Bettin actually looks a lot like his creation. He's svelte. His head is mostly bare and he has a distinct jaw line. In conversation, he speaks precisely, with an understated confidence. He's self-conscious about his English—about as self-conscious as I should be about my German—but he can eloquently describe the Kwiggle's properties in either language. When I send him some written questions, his letter back comes to 2,500 words, easily the longest and most effusive response I've ever received to an email interview.

Bettin grew up in Wolfsburg, a city best known as the headquarters of the Volkswagen motor company. Volkswagen dominates the town, and much of Bettin's family has worked there. Bettin earned his degree in mechanical engineering from the Braunschweig Technical Institute in 1993 and worked in the field for more than two decades before incorporating Kwiggle around 2015.

Alongside Bettin is his son, Till, who has helped with the Kwiggle's development and become a partner in the business. Till has helped with design details, training new workers, and quality control. He currently manages a team of ten builders and coordinates with thirty-five different suppliers.

Once Bettin was satisfied with his R&D, Kwiggle won widespread attention in a most 21st century way—by crowdfunding. Kwiggle was a darling on Kickstarter and received a series of write ups in English-language websites, which mostly praised its unusual design and compact fold.

This attention reached its zenith in 2019, when the Kwiggle debuted on a television series, *Das Ding des Jahres*, or *The Thing of the Year*. On the show, contestants showcase their inventions for a live audience. Karsten and Till appeared on the program, and Till showed off both the folding mechanism and its rideability. The Kwiggle earned a lot of applause; the judges even volunteered to ride two Kwiggle bikes through the studio, demonstrating how quick the "wiggle" technique was to learn.

For people like me, who needed some time to grasp what the Kwiggle actually was, the televised exposure was a major boost. The YouTube version alone received nearly 200,000 views.

Today, Kwiggle is an established business, and it's growing. Customers can order their own Kwiggle from the official website. Units can be delivered almost anywhere in the European Union, and they have gained a widespread continental following.

More personally, Bettin has seen people riding the Kwiggle around his home city of Hanover, Germany, where the company is headquartered. Bettin jokes that he knew Kwiggle was a success when he spotted strangers, and not friends or family members, riding them.

In my rusty German, I offer Bettin a similar example: I'm a published author, and every once in a while, I will spot my own book on the shelf of a bookstore. This accidental encounter is followed by a very distinct kind of joy.

Bettin smiles. "Yes," he says. "It's something like that."

Stronger, Faster, Farther

It's easy to think of the Kwiggle as just a nifty machine. After all, Bettin has more than answered his initial question: *Can you invent a bike that you ride standing up?* The answer is, in a word, *yes.*

But Bettin's curiosity has grown along with his invention. At 57 years old, he considers himself a fit but unexceptional rider: once a week, he rides about 65 kilometers, plus intermittent exercise. Until recently, his longest ride was 150 kilometers, just short of 100 miles, the coveted "century" in the English system.

Yet Bettin believes that the Kwiggle's ergonomic design makes it possible to ride extremely long distances, and he's endeavored to prove this himself. First, he rode around the IJsselmeer, a substantial body of water in the Netherlands. Over the course of sixteen hours, Bettin pedaled 300 kilometers.

"Amazingly, I was then able to ride long stretches at a time, even with headwinds, before I needed a break," he tells me. "And even more amazingly, I restarted after breaks as if I were just starting the tour. All in all, a fantastic experience."

Two hundred miles is an astonishing distance, even for Iron Man competitors, never mind soft spoken German engineers. Like most of the Low Countries, the IJsselmeer is fairly flat. He needed a steeper test, so Bettin tried a fourteen-kilometer ride through the Alps, at an elevation of 1,000 meters. First he rode a racing bicycle, then he rode the same segment on a Kwiggle. The ascent was much smoother, he writes in his blog. Then there was the descent: he accelerated to 55 kmh, or roughly 35 mph, in what he playfully described as "slalom mode." Such velocity would be considered fast on a regular road bike, never mind a folding bike with eight-inch wheels.

"My most fantastic cycling experience ever," he wrote.

Bettin has the favoritism of an inventor, of course, and two dramatic rides hardly qualify as settled science. But Bettin is striving for something even more ambitious than a bike you can stand on: he wants the Kwiggle to rival, or even surpass, the traditional bicycle.

American Dream

I have never seen a Kwiggle in real life.

Up till now, units haven't been widely available in the United States. My only exposure consists of JPGs and video clips on the Internet.

But that's about to change. Bettin expects to enter the U.S. market. To start, the company will ship its product directly from Germany. But it's very possible that Kwiggle will open a brick-and-mortar store in a major American city, or even several. Other folding bike brands, like Brompton and Dahon, have flagship stores in (among other places) New York City. Bettin is interested in a distributor, or even a partnership. For now, it's all up in the air.

Despite its benefits, Kwiggle isn't exactly an easy sell. You have to like the stripped-down aesthetic and unusual riding position. You can't expect an electric upgrade anytime soon. And you must be willing to shell out €1,280, or about $1,500. That's a big impulse buy for something that has never been seen, much less ridden, on American roads.

I'm also fairly cynical about bicycling in my native country. I have ridden large chunks of Western Europe, including parts of the Rhine and Ruhr Rivers, across Belgium and the French *campagne*, and the experience is night and day. Europe isn't a two-wheeled Utopia, but Europeans are—literally—miles ahead of Americans in terms of cycling culture. The Kwiggle would look eccentric anywhere, and it has yet to receive the glare of, say, a tattooed American contractor in a Ford pickup, who wants to share the road with exactly no one.

But the perception is rapidly changing. Small-wheeled bikes are everywhere now. Electric scooters zip down American sidewalks, moving every kind of person around with unironic ease. Many U.S. cities have a bike-share program, and where it exists, it's popular. Bikes are more diverse than ever, and they're better accepted every day.

And it's hard not to get swept up in Bettin's enthusiasm. During our conversation over Zoom, we struggle to communicate, each searching for the right words in the other's language. Still, excitement simmers under Bettin's every sentence. After ten years of meticulous work, Kwiggle has become his full-time job, and this odd little experiment is about to cross the ocean.

"I think America is very big," says Bettin, "and there are so many different people with different interests and preferences and so many uses for this compact folding bike: commuters, city travelers, parking lot seekers, sailors, sport flyers, boaters, fitness enthusiasts and many more.

"My conviction has always been that if I do something that helps a lot of people and brings them real benefits and maybe contributes to a better world, then business success will follow," he adds. "If I had only wanted to make a business decision, I would have been better off doing other things like developing apps or something like that. I have enough ideas. In the end, though, it is important that you do something that corresponds to your deep inner conviction."

Rack 'Em

I DIDN'T HAVE far to drive. A couple miles, maybe. All I had to do was park in a driveway, meet my friend Mike, throw his bike on my rack, and carpool over to the Neponset trailhead.

But as my Subaru turned onto a bridge, and motorists jockeyed for position all around me, I sensed that something was wrong. A slight vibration. A hint of sound. An anomaly in the rearview mirror. I might have ignored it. But that's when I heard a car horn; a driver leaned out of his window, jabbing a finger at my rear bumper.

I pulled onto the shoulder and threw open the door. Cars flew past. Rounding the trunk, I saw my rack, which carried both our bikes—sort of. The straps were stretched out; the bikes dipped low. Mike's eyes widened at the sight of his hybrid tires, which nearly touched the ground. Another inch or two lower, and the pavement would have ripped the bikes right off.

"Huh," I said—or rather yelled over the wail of passing cars. "Well, that was close."

I emptied the rack, tightened the straps, and affixed the bikes once more. They looked secure, but then again, they *always* looked secure. I gritted my teeth as we merged with traffic once more.

This is killing me, I thought. *Why the hell isn't it working? That rack is literally* designed *for two bikes.*

And then a second thought, far less indignant, burbled up from my subconscious. *Dude, come on— you get what you pay for.*

My Thule Cents

Two years have passed since that close call in Quincy, Massachusetts. But the memory is still fresh, and I'm forever grateful that I didn't destroy both our bikes in one fell swoop. I also learned my lesson: never overload an Allen Sports Deluxe Two-Bike Trunk Mount. Nothing good can happen if you do.

At this moment, I'm in the market for a new car. Well, a not a *new* car, but a dependably used one. And because my wife knows me so well, she says, "Whatever we get, let's make sure we add a trailer hitch. Because you *need* a good bike rack."

I'm excited about this prospect. At last, a rack that doesn't cleave to the fissures of my car with a few blunt hooks. Never again will I entrust my most precious possession to a handful of nylon bands. How great will it be, to open my hatch without also lifting ten extra pounds of metal frame, as its rigging dangles everywhere? In short, I will soon upgrade—from a janky little bike rack I bought off Amazon for about $30, to a bona fide Thule.

Thule Group AB is a manufacturing company based in Sweden. If you're into bikes at all, you probably see that name everywhere, printed in bold white letters. The company has been crafting "sports carriers" since 1962, and the moment you approach a national park, you see SUV after SUV outfitted with Thule racks. The company makes all kinds of racks—roof racks, hitch racks, racks for one bike or even four—and they're considered the gold standard for safe transport of your bike. Thule makes a range of other things, too, like backpacks, strollers, hard cases, you name it. Their tagline: "Bring your life."

I can't wait to attach a hypothetical Thule to my hypothetical car. And I will happily settle for a decent knock-off. A trailer hitch is many times more dependable than the clumsy little rack I've used.

But there's something unsettling about this upgrade. A bike rack is a very public kind of sports equipment. I'm not just graduating to a better gadget. I am announcing—for anyone on the Interstate to see—that I have moved from one social class to another.

Keeping Up with the Thules

In the United States, it's perfectly normal *not* to bike from Point A to Point B.

If Point A is your house, and you want to go out for a leisurely ride, odds are you won't do this in your own neighborhood. You may live on a steep hill. Local traffic may be aggressive. You're lucky to have bike lanes, or a decent shoulder, or even sidewalks. You may face potholes or endless construction. The list of roadblocks is endless.

So, you may very well *start* your bike-ride at Point B. This place could be anywhere—a park, a path, a peaceful lake, a giant parking lot. Your ideal Point B may even lie in another county or state. Wherever it is, Point B is probably pleasant and bike-friendly. *And* a healthy distance from your front door.

There's nothing "wrong" with this—we like what we like, and we'd rather be safe than sorry. But it does mean that a bicycle, a machine used for land transportation, requires another machine to transport it overland to the place where it's safe enough transport *you*. We may spend more time just driving our bikes to a trailhead than we do actually biking.

If you have a Thule, life is a breeze. Toss a few bikes on its sturdy frame, and drive your Ford Escape wherever you want to go. A riverside path? Sure! Yellowstone National Park? No problem! A properly installed Thule is one of the most dependable things you can put on your car.

This may be more essential now than ever. Ebikes can easily weigh fifty to eighty pounds. The battery alone feels like a brick, and the frames are bulky. Only a quality rack has the muscle you need; a Thule can carry even the huskiest ebike. Which is reassuring, if you spent more on your Juggernaut Ultra Beast 2 than you did on your first car.

There's just one hitch—literally, the trailer hitch, which costs hundreds of dollars to install, plus the rack itself. You can get away with a decent two-bike Thule for, say, $200, but if you don't already have a hitch attached to your chassis, the combined price tag may be uncomfortable.

The same goes for roof racks. If you already have a roof rack, great. If not—the whole enterprise gets expensive, fast.

So what if you don't have $500 to spend on your weekend pastime, but you still want to carpool with your friend Mike in Quincy, Massachusetts? That's when you invest $30 in an Allen Sports Deluxe Two-Bike Trunk Mount. Which may work perfectly well for hundreds of miles; but also, you may hit a speed bump, the rack will collapse, and your rims will be totally destroyed. Who knows?

Even cheap racks may be too great a commitment to actually buy. I've loaned my second-rate Allen rack to friends on several occasions, attaching it to a range of hatchbacks and sedans. These trips were short, usually to a mechanic or nearby park. To me, the Allen rack is an embarrassing last resort. To my friends, the Allen rack is far better than what they have, which is nothing.

Before I had the rack, I *also* had nothing. I'd whip off the front wheel and jam my bike into any vehicle that would fit it. I used trunks and flatbeds, back seats and lowered front seats, any space I could claim without tearing the upholstery. And this was all assuming I could find a vehicle to use, which, for much of life, wasn't a sure thing.

There's one bright spot, and that is the city bus. I ride mass transit as often as I can. Every single RIPTA bus in Rhode Island is outfitted with a two-bike rack on the front. They're durable and easy to use, and they cost nothing extra. This is standard practice in cities across the U.S., and it's something to celebrate.

Still, there are limits. If I had taken public transit to visit my friend Mike in Quincy, it would have taken me nearly three hours just to get there—and cost about $40 round-trip.

Getting Hitched

At the car dealership, I sign a stack of papers. The dealer is a big, dopey guy named Brian. In a few minutes, Brian will screw a temporary license to our new/used car and my wife and I will drive away.

So much of buying a car is sitting around and waiting, and the only distraction is a rerun of *Two and a Half Men* playing on the lobby TV. As we wait for a fax from our insurance company, I try to make small talk with Brian.

"I'm glad this finally worked out," I say. "We've been looking for a replacement car for awhile."

"Yeah," Brian says, swinging his arms playfully. "I'm glad you nailed down this price. We got another one in just like it, and it's selling for twice as much."

"The market's been crazy," I add. "But I guess I don't have to tell *you* that."

"Yeah," Brian says again, now clapping his hands with each swing. "I don't get it."

I balk. Does he *really* not get it, or is that just something to say? Ever since the pandemic started, the automotive market has been a rollercoaster; tens of millions of drivers lost their jobs; must-have computer chips have been in short supply. My wife and I returned our second car—a lease—several months early, just because it was a needless liability in the middle of a lockdown. At this moment, new cars are scarce and prices are sky-high. If we hadn't found a deal, we wouldn't have sprung for a second vehicle, at least not now. The long-term costs would have been absurd.

But I don't say any of this to Brian. The last thing he needs is negativity, especially from a rando customer who resents driving at all.

Instead, I browse the bike racks on display. There are several, all of them designed for trailer hitches.

"Yeah," says Brian again, "these are pretty great. Once we put on that hitch, you're gonna have a lot of options."

I smile. A part of me is heartened. It's great to know how popular cycling has become, that bike racks are prominently displayed on the showroom floor. For a generic dealership in the middle of a Rhode Island suburb, the Thules say a lot about what modern consumers want. True, a trailer hitch can be used for a lot of useful things—including, say, an actual trailer. And yes, it's a not-small investment. But I like to think of it as a step in the right direction.

"They look awesome," I say to Brian. "I can't wait."

WHEELS OF FREEDOM

I'm picturing a movie.

In the opening scene, Kittie Knox threads a needle. She sits at a workbench in a cramped little shop. Fabrics are draped all around her, and headless mannequins wear half-made dresses. Kittie licks the thread, but she's having trouble pushing it through the needle's eye. As she concentrates, something flashes past the window.

Kittie looks up. Did she see something go by? Or was it a trick of the light? She shakes it off and goes back to her work.

A second later, the same flash. A circular blur.

"Kittie!" calls another seamstress. "Come over!"

Kittie scampers across the shop and leans out the door. There is a hubbub outside; onlookers line the sidewalk. Morning light bathes the cobblestone. And there, silhouetted against the golden sun, a man straddles a penny-farthing. The enormous front wheel rolls beneath his polished shoes. He rides in circles, smiling brightly. Spectators point and murmur. He doffs his pork pie hat, and people in the crowd clap excitedly.

"What is it?" someone cries.

The man laughs. "Why this here," he calls back, "is what they call a *bicycle*."

Kittie watches the man.

"A bicycle," she whispers.

"Just look at that there contraption!" exclaims her fellow seamstress. "Looks like somebody broke a buggy in half. Can you imagine riding one of them things? Somebody'd have to be crazy!"

But Kittie keeps watching. Because she's enchanted. One way or another, she's going to find a bicycle, and she's going to ride it.

And yet—the audience wonders how this could possibly happen. From their costumes, this scene clearly takes place in the late 19th century. Kittie is a woman. Actually, she's a girl, probably 12 or 13 years old. That alone would make her journey seem unlikely. But there's something else, something we notice the moment Kittie appears onscreen. Kittie isn't just a Victorian female. She's also black.

A Ride of Her Own

It should be obvious why I want this movie to exist. Katherine Knox was one of the first African-American women ever to own a bicycle, much less race one, much less win many of those races. Her life is ripe for adaptation—a strong-willed woman of color who countered every expectation of her era.

And the drama starts right away, as Kittie saves for years to afford her own bicycle. In an early montage, Kittie walks to work, through rain and sleet. First, a single bicycle passes her, then another. They are high-wheelers, just like the one she saw. She grows older, and she passes more cyclists—a pair, a trio, then a whole group of them. The bikes get smaller, more familiar. In her kitchen, Kittie pulls out a coffee tin, where the bundles of money multiply. At last, as Kittie turns twenty, the tin is full of cash. It is clear how much this bike will cost, and how disciplined is her saving.

At last, the day arrives. A caption reads: "1893." Kittie gingerly steps into a bike shop. The shopkeeper is a youthful white man with a waxed mustache. He looks surprised to see her there. At first, the shopkeeper mistakes her for a missionary, or maybe a housekeeper looking for work. Then she says, "I'd like to buy a bicycle, sir."

The shopkeeper isn't sure what to do. He shows her a number of used bicycles, rusty and battered. But Kittie looks past the rows of wheels and frames, right to the back, where she spots her prize: a shiny new "safety" bicycle, with equally sized wheels and a leather seat. She tiptoes toward the bike, trembling with reverence.

"Top of the line," proclaims the shopkeeper. "And costs a pretty penny, I might add."

Kittie faces the shopkeeper. "How pretty?"

"That one here costs a hundred dollars, even."

Kittie reaches into her bag and produces a wad of cash. "Sold."

First Attempt

Then comes the next challenge: how does a Boston seamstress, dressed in corset and layers of skirts, even mount a bicycle saddle? Kittie wheels her new machine into a city park. She looks around, self-conscious. A couple of old men watch her from a nearby bench; they whisper and chuckle.

Kittie tries to pull herself onto the saddle, but she tumbles over. She brushes herself off, then scowls. (The men are openly laughing now). The next try, the bike moves, but she skips along on one foot; the handlebars shake in her hands. Kittie falls forward and pants in place. She tries a few more times, but she just can't make it work.

Flashback!

Kittie remembers a moment from her girlhood, in the same park, when she was playing with a hoop and stick. She tries to roll the hoop, but it keeps falling over. Then a friend comes over, pigtailed and wise. The friend says: "You gotta keep it moving! The faster it goes, the better it rolls!"

Kittie goes back to the bike. She presses her leather boot against the pedal. She bundles her petticoats. She takes a deep breath. Then she pushes down, hard. The bike rolls. She looks shocked at first, but her feet start to rotate. The bike zigzags, but it stays in motion. Kittie pedals the bike down the pavement. Picnickers look up. She rides faster, straighter. She rounds the park.

In a moment of triumph, she passes the two old men, who are now cheering her on. She beams with joy. And then she mumbles, "Now, how do you stop this thing?"

She squeezes the brakes, and the bike awkwardly lurches to a halt. Kittie bends over, pressing her head into the handlebars. She's sweating. She's exasperated. But she also smiles.

If you're wondering, all this backstory is made up. Knox didn't keep a diary, as far as I know. She appeared in numerous articles, but she wasn't so much quoted as *described*. Knox had little ownership over her own story, and a historian can only guess her innermost thoughts. We barely know what she looked like; only a handful of photos exist.

From a screenwriting perspective, that's great. There is a lot of room to imagine Knox's life, to illustrate her mastery of the bicycle.

As she struggles in her Gilded Age attire, Kittie whispers curses at her skirts, which keep getting caught up in the gears. When she arrives at work, her coworkers giggle at the chain-grease staining her hem. At the end of her shift, Kittie is about to go home, but then she notices a pile of spare fabric in the corner. She measures it out, cuts and sews, until she has pieced together her own bloomers. Night has fallen outside, and lamps are now lit in the darkened shop. Kittie steps into their warm glow and admires her work in the mirror. They hang loose around her legs and boots, like jodhpurs.

The next thing we see, Kittie is weaving through Boston foot-traffic in her sporty new outfit. Heads turn wherever she goes. She rides farther and faster. She joins clusters of other riders, mostly white and male, who are startled by her presence.

A friendly young cyclist calls out, "You ought to join our club!"

"Club?" Kittie calls back.

"The League of American Wheelmen!"

Which is a turning point in our story, because now Kittie wants nothing more than to join the LAW, to rub shoulders with folks who understand her obsession. She will share pavement with the slickest cyclists in the country.

Or so she thinks.

Ups and Downs

Every Cinderella story requires a good villain, and this movie has a perfect antagonist: Mary Sargent Hopkins, publisher of *The Wheelwoman Magazine*.

At first glance, Hopkins is a stiff and dignified woman. She pours herself tea in a cozy Victorian parlor. She flips through her own magazine, scanning the articles through a pair of pince-nez.

Then she turns to a copy of the *Boston Globe*, where she sees a tiny article: "NEGRESS JOINS WHEELMEN."

Hopkins recoils in horror. There, beneath the headline, is an etched illustration: a young, confident, African-American woman posing beside her safety bicycle.

A maid enters the room. "Would you care for anything, Ma'am?"

Hopkins scoffs. She jabs a finger into the paper. "Disgraceful," she declares. "If there is one thing I hate, it is a masculine woman."

For the rest of the film, Hopkins does everything she can to discredit Kittie. She runs opinion pieces. She tells reporters to write unflattering coverage. She commissions racist cartoons. She gossips at parties.

At one point, Hopkins speaks at a suffragette rally. She delivers a speech about voting rights, and the crowd claps. A moderator, wearing a sash and enormous feathered hat, asks the crowd if they have any questions.

"What about Kittie Knox?" someone calls out.

Hopkins sours visibly. "What about her?"

"Oughtn't she be allowed into bicycle clubs?"

Hopkins raises her nose. "All I can say is this: she can't be a man, and she is a disgrace as a woman. If Kittie Knox wants to dress like a Turk, she should put on the veil as well."

Still, Hopkins can't stop Kittie's rise to fame, nor can anyone else.

Kittie enters her first race with the Wheelmen, a 100-mile ride across Martha's Vineyard. We watch her fly down scenic country roads, along the winding coast, passing male riders as she goes. She rides with stoic confidence. When she crosses the finish line, a bearded man approaches to shake her hand.

"You've won, Miss Knox!" he proclaims.

"I have?"

"First place, in the women's category!"

Kittie lets this sink in. "How'd I do overall?"

The man offers an avuncular smile. "Better than anyone imagined."

More races; more glory; more accolades from fellow members. Men ride with her in public. They hold doors for her. Recurring characters reveal her growing circle of friends. Reporters watch her from the press box, furiously scribbling into their notebooks.

Then it all grinds to a halt: Kittie arrives at a race, ready to show her stuff. But a bunch of men approach, blocking her way.

"Sorry, Kittie," snickers one. "New rule. *No coloreds allowed.*"

Kittie is gobsmacked. She can't believe it. But the charter has in fact changed: no non-white people can be inducted into the League of American Wheelmen.

"This isn't right," declares Kittie. And she will spend the rest of the movie proving her case.

Well-Behaved Women Rarely Make History

The third act practically writes itself. Kittie's supporters notice a loophole in the new law: *no non-whites may join as members* doesn't mean that *current* non-white members are no longer allowed. Allies insist that Kittie can stay; enemies argue that her friends are just splitting hairs. Harsh words are exchanged; fights break out; dramatic headlines are printed.

Kittie soldiers on. She goes to New Jersey, where she plans to attend the League's annual conference. She arrives at a beautiful seaside mansion. Crowds of cyclists are already gathered there, smoking pipes and showing off their steeds. As Kittie nears the main entrance, the men go quiet. Tension fills the air. Kittie reaches the veranda and presents her membership card.

The doorman sneers. "You, miss, seem to be at the wrong house."

No one breathes a word.

Kittie can't force her way in. So she swallows her anger, shoots the doorman a scathing look, and wheels her bike away.

But then something happens: another Wheelman grabs his bike and follows hers.

Then another, and another.

Scores of Wheelmen vacate the building, where they should be mingling and sipping brandy.

This is the movie's tearjerker moment, when half the League's members ride away from their now-racist institution, pedaling alongside Kittie in a massive show of solidarity. They roll down the road, triumphant in their numbers. In the streets of Asbury Park, passersby cheer the impromptu parade.

(I almost don't want to tell you that this isn't remotely what happened that day. True, most League members opposed the new rule and supported Knox's membership. But when Knox was turned away at the door, she almost certainly left on her own. These riders were members of polite society and would never think to do something so radical, no matter what their personal feelings. But movies are fantasies, after all).

Reparations

The League finally caves. The next evening, Kittie is allowed to attend a Wheelmen gala. Now we see a hint of romance: Kittie arrives in her finest gown, and the tuxedoed cyclists—every one of them white—ask Kittie to dance. In a nearly wordless montage, the many patrons whirl around the floor with her, admiring her dignity and hitherto unrecognized beauty. For one solitary evening, Kittie is (literally) the belle of the ball.

At last, the finale: a century ride through Massachusetts.

True to history, a thunderstorm rages all around. Rain pours.

Untrue to history, the movie should end with a showdown between Kittie and one of her rivals—some aristocratic bigot who has dogged her since the beginning. Kittie pedals furiously down muddy roads, her homemade garments drenched, her crank arms squeaking with every turn. The race really happened, but this specific rivalry is made up; we can make up whatever we want. Does the rival fall into a river, requiring her aid? Does he attempt to cheat, by ramming a cudgel into her spokes? Like any good sports movie, this story should conclude with symbolic gestures. Finally, Kittie triumphs. She is the only woman to complete the race. She crosses the finish line, to the applause of friends and fans. *Freeze frame!*

Before the credits roll, we see a few epilogues about the characters and their legacy:

"*The Wheelwoman* magazine ceased publication soon after."

"The League of American Wheelmen was renamed the League of American Bicyclists. The 'color bar' was finally removed from its bylaws more than a century later."

"Kittie Knox died of kidney disease in 1900, at the age of 26. The Kittie Knox Bike Path was dedicated in 2019."

Herstory

Knox's story isn't well known. When I browsed the Internet for books about her life, the only meaningful title came from a series, *Bicycle Culture Rising*, by activist and entrepreneur Joe Biel. This little chapbook is thoroughly researched and well put together; archival photos help illustrate Knox's life and times. It's a remarkable little treatise, which goes on to explain the lasting significance of the color bar controversy.

Like all biopics, my movie would be full of errors and exaggerations. Major events would be condensed into digestible scenes. Many real people are combined into a few fictional characters. Difficult choices must be made: Do we learn that Kittie has a black father and white mother? Do we ever meet her brother? Does the 100-minute run-time allow for a speculative love story? And what will happen after a focus group or two? A Hollywood studio will manipulate the story in embarrassing ways, miscasting actors and cutting all the best moments, until the cinematic Kittie Knox would be unrecognizable to the real one.

But the most important themes would remain intact: Knox was a powerful athlete. She fought hard for equal rights. And she used the bicycle—a faddish new technology—as a tool for empowerment and self-expression.

No movie could do Knox's life justice, any more than *Harriet* could live up to the actual Harriet Tubman or *Selma* could sum up Dr. King. But her story aches to be adapted. Its relevance to today's world is frustratingly clear. And for some reason, I have this feeling that Kittie would've loved it.

Bamboo Revolution

Kwabena Danso didn't grow up riding bicycles. When Danso was a kid, there weren't many bikes around. Some were available for rent, so neighbors could run errands around the village, but Danso's family couldn't afford even that small luxury. And anyway, it took him years for the chance to even learn.

"I knew very little about bikes," Danso told me recently over Zoom. "I learned to ride a bicycle when I was fifteen or sixteen years."

In college, Danso studied psychology. Later, he earned an MBA in Business Administration. But for all those years, bicycles were the last thing on his mind. He didn't go on extravagant tours. He didn't bomb down mountains. He didn't apprentice in a repair shop to put himself through school.

And yet—cycling has become a pillar of his life. Kwabena Danso is the founder and CEO of Booomers Bicycles, based in the African nation of Ghana. To Danso, the bicycle isn't just sports equipment; it's a holistic education. It's an economic powerhouse. It's a business model based on health and sustainability. And above all, it's a chance to raise rural Ghanaians out of poverty, so the next generation doesn't have to grow up the way he did.

And at the center of it all is the Booomers Bike—slick, beautiful, and made of bamboo.

Interventions

Danso grew up in the village of Yonso, in rural Ghana. The village is home to only 500 people, and most of them live in poverty. As a kid, Danso had little access to books and often went hungry. He was able to pay for school, thanks to his grandfather, who worked in the United Kingdom and sent money home. But Danso's humble origins weighed on him, even as an undergraduate at the University of Ghana.

Eventually, Danso started seeing a counselor, to help him work through his emotional issues. During an early session, the counselor told Danso to go home and think about some fundamental questions. *What did he like to do? What were his talents? What would ultimately make him happy?*

"I came home, sat down," Danso tells me, "and the one thing I really saw I was happy to be doing was helping people. Helping people solve their problems. Trying to support others. And that was when, at the same time, I realized my community has so many difficulties. A lot of children don't have enough food. A lot of women are economically unempowered, and they live at the mercy of their husbands. And so, a lot of things go wrong."

This was a watershed moment for Danso, and for the many people he would soon encounter. In 2005, Danso helped create a special awards program for outstanding students and teachers in Yonso. The ceremony was meant to promote education and achievement in a community that is desperately underserved. Danso met exchange students from the University of Vermont, and they worked together to start a book drive.

From there, the idea snowballed. Danso is now executive director of the Yonso Project, a nonprofit organization headquartered in his hometown. He's forty-one years old, and he's been working to improve conditions in Yonso for nearly half his lifetime.

The Yonso Project still promotes reading and education, but it also provides scholarships for underprivileged students. And because the job market is especially challenging for Ghanaian women, the Yonso Project offers microloans to female entrepreneurs, along with rigorous business training. At last count, Yonso had provided more than $40,000 in loans. To put this in perspective, the per capita income in Ghana is a little more than $2,000 per year, or about $5 per day.

By 2009, these were the kinds of things Kwabena Danso was doing. He was a mover and shaker. He was building up his community. But he wasn't exactly a businessman. He hadn't started studying his MBA, which would come later. And he still knew almost nothing about bicycles.

Then he met Craig Calfee, and everything changed.

Bamboo Guru

Danso didn't really know who he was meeting. All he knew was that an American named Craig Calfee had built a bicycle out of bamboo, and he was teaching people in Africa to build them as well.

"When my friend Sam told me, I was like, 'Are you joking? No way. Until I see it, I'm not going to believe it,'" remembers Danso.

But in the bicycle industry, Calfee is a legend. He's built carbon-fiber frames since 1987, and his bikes have competed in the Tour de France. His company, Calfee Design, has been involved in all sorts of creative engineering, including a James Bond-caliber motorcycle that converts into a gyrocopter. A whole book could be written about Craig Calfee and his unlikely exploits.

Like Danso, Calfee also had a watershed moment. He described it in an interview for *Smithsonian Magazine:*

> *"One afternoon, in 1995, my dog Luna and I started playing with a bamboo stick. I was sure it would break, or splinter—but it didn't. I'd never realized how strong bamboo was. It inspired me, and I built my first bamboo bike as a gimmick for a trade show."*

Gimmick or not, conventiongoers were genuinely impressed with the prototype. Once the trade show was over, Calfee wondered whether bamboo bicycles might have a real future.

As it happens, Calfee already had a relationship with Africa. He had traveled parts of the continent during the 1980s, and he had some familiarity with the quality of life in nations like Ghana. In 2006, he started a collaboration with the Earth Institute, a division of Columbia University, to train African workers to build bamboo bike frames. The result was Bamboosero, an initiative designed to do just that.

Cottage Industry

Danso first heard of Calfee through a mutual friend, an American named Sam Dupre, who was one of the exchange students from UVM and a founding member of the Yonso Project. When Danso saw the bikes firsthand, he was astonished. All his incredulity melted in a single day.

"Lo and behold, we saw the bike, and I was amazed with what I saw," he says. "I'm like, 'Wow.' And the first thing that came into my mind is, this is a huge potential opportunity in Ghana, because we have a lot of bamboo."

Ghana *does* have a lot of bamboo. It also had a large, underused workforce. Sure, even a bamboo bicycle needs a lot of metal components, but the bike itself can be assembled anywhere. You don't need to deal with engines, forges, CAD systems, or CNC machines. Builders don't need degrees in engineering. The whole operation can take place in a rustic environment—like Yonso, Ghana.

Danso may not have been a lifelong cyclist, but the promise was clear. If Calfee could lay the groundwork, Danso could hire local workers. He could build a factory—*not* in a big industrial town, but in Yonso, where jobs had always been scarce.

There was only one question: Could Danso manage both projects at the same time? Could he serve as executive director of a badly needed nonprofit *and* break ground on a startup company? Could he be responsible for scholarships and micro-financing while, at the same time, making sure that bike-builders were fully trained in a brand-new skill?

"It took me like a year to make that decision," he says. "I had to look at the implications of having a for-profit company and all the things that you need to do—in addition to a nonprofit."

In the end, of course, Danso said yes.

The Bamboo Advantage

I first heard about bamboo bicycles from my Dad, during one of our idle afternoon conversations. My Dad has always been interested in engine-less gadgets and green technology, and naturally he knew about this.

A bamboo bike might sound a little strange, he told me, but it really made a lot of sense. Bamboo is light and durable. It biodegrades easily. He'd even heard of special kits, designed so regular people could assemble their own.

I loved this idea, in theory. Here's a plant that sprouts all over the world. Bamboo is fast-growing and resilient. The hollow shafts bear such a striking resemblance to frame tubes that it's almost hard to believe. Bamboo absorbs vibrations, so it's actually good for high-impact activities like gravel riding. Bamboo has long been used for furniture and irrigation; why couldn't you fashion a bike out of it, too?

This idea is so intuitive that two inventors, August Oberg and Andrew Gustafson, patented the first known bamboo bicycle in 1896. At that time, the "safety bicycle" had only really existed for 10 years. Bamboo never became popular, and it will always be a niche market. But the *potential* for bamboo bikes has never waned.

Fast-forward to the 21st Century, when "sustainability" is on the tip of everyone's tongue, and bamboo is used in ways Oberg and Gustafson could never have imagined. You can buy bamboo pillows and bamboo toilet paper, bamboo straws and bamboo pet collars. Bamboo has become the superfood of construction materials, and numerous bike-makers have jumped on the opportunity.

And my Dad was right: there *are* DIY kits that enable you—like *you*, reading this—to build your own bamboo bike from the ground up. There's the Bamboo Bicycle Club, founded by a Londoner named James Marr in 2012.

And there's also Calfee Design—founded by the same Craig Calfee who showed Danso how to build them in rural Ghana. If you're willing to spend the time and money, Calfee Design will send you all the tools, materials, and schematics you need to create a bamboo bike at home.

There are plenty of differences between bamboo and metal frames, but the big one is this: you can't weld bamboo together; the torch would incinerate your frame. Instead, a craftsman uses fibers to bind the tubes into a proper angle. For Calfee, hemp did the trick. The hemp twine is saturated in an epoxy, which hardens into a solid, immovable joint.

Technically, bamboo isn't as strong as most metals; but for everyday cyclists, it'll withstand the usual stresses. According to that same Smithsonian interview, Calfee once commissioned four men to combine their weight and break his frame. What ended up breaking wasn't the bamboo, but the metal wheels.

The Next Generation

Booomers Bamboo Bikes is a thriving business, and Danso is doing very well. But it's hard to overstate how much Booomers is thriving, and the impact it's having on rural Ghana—and the world.

The stats alone are astonishing: Danso employs forty full-time workers, who assemble the frames on-site. Workers earn a competitive wage and health benefits, plus a complimentary lunch each workday. Booomers relies on 200 farmers in the region, who cultivate the bamboo itself. At last count, the company has sold more than 3,000 bike frames.

Booomers is closely tied to the Yonso Project. Through his foundation, Danso has been able to donate 150 of his bikes to local schools, and 15 percent of every sale goes to Yonso. This money has helped fund scholarships, libraries, and even computer labs. It helped fund the Yonso Project Model School, an ambitious modern campus that educates more than 200 children.

Most Booomers customers live in Europe, but the company has started selling in North America as well. The website is plastered in quotes and snapshots from customers, who have used the bamboo bikes to take long-distance tours.

And Danso himself has won a lot of attention. He's given many interviews, for the likes of the BBC and Voice of America. He's received many honors, including a Global Fellowship Award for Social Entrepreneurs from the International Youth Foundation. He partners with several other organizations, including UNICEF.

So yes, Danso may have discovered cycling late in life, but he knows how much a bicycle can teach a young rider.

"I feel like if I had known the benefits of riding earlier, it would have been more helpful," he reflects. "I would have been used to biking. I would have become accustomed to the purchase, so it would become part and parcel of my life. I think that, if children start cycling, they get to learn a lot about the things that keep them healthy, that keep them fit. It also saves them a lot of money, and it's also part of the environment. These were things I didn't know, and I wish I knew them when I was young."

Today, those lessons extend to his own children.

"My kids are right now around seven, eight, five," he says, "and they are riding already."

War Machine?

When the video opens, a soldier stands on the edge of an open doorway. He wears goggles and an olive uniform. He looks like your standard paratrooper, readying himself to leap out of a plane and parachute into checkered fields several thousand feet below.

But as he maneuvers to the edge, we see the equipment strapped to his chest: two overlapping wheels and a frame. Sunbeams spill over his face as the soldier peers down, into the empty air. He falls forward, bike and all. The video fades to black.

This was my first glimpse of the Montague Paratrooper, a folding mountain bike that had popped up on Google. I'd been flirting with mountain bikes ever since my son had expressed an interest in taking on more rugged terrain. A folding design appealed to me, as it always does, and my first search led to Montague.

Huh, I thought. *I wonder why they call it "The Paratrooper."*

This promo video, embedded on the Montague website, makes the name clear: the bike was created for actual paratroopers. These bikes can apparently be taken on military operations. The Paratrooper not only folds to half its size; it can be fastened to an actual soldier and dropped into combat zones.

Is this for real? I wondered. *Does the army actually use bicycles?*

The Pros

Let's go back in time, to the 1890s.

Imagine you are a general at war, or at least a general preparing for war. For now, cast aside your notions of peace and diplomacy. You must defeat your enemies, at all costs. Your era is known for mounted cavalry and breech-loading rifles. You are looking for the latest technological advantage: dynamite, Gatling guns, ironclad warships. And one day, someone approaches you with a bicycle.

You see a lot of potential in this little machine. It's light and fast. Unlike a horse, the bike doesn't have to be bred or trained. It's ready for action the moment it rolls off the factory line, and your nation can build as many as it needs. Your cadets may never have pedaled a bicycle, but they can learn in a few days. Bikes are light and easy to store. With the right racks and panniers, troops can affix their kits and bedrolls. Compared to marching on foot, riding is a breeze.

Bikes are also quiet. They won't whinny or neigh. Loud noises won't spook them. They require no fuel, beyond the food a soldier will eat anyway. Every part can be replaced, and the same model could change hands for years. The bike is a seductive means of getting men and materiel into position. Speed and mobility are of the essence. In the 1890s, no transport on Earth was more efficient.

Where the Buffalo Soldiers Roam

This was the reasoning of Second Lieutenant James A. Moss, an army officer who had freshly graduated from West Point. Moss was already an enthusiastic wheelman, so it's little surprise that he dreamed of turning his regiment, the 25th Infantry, into the first American "Bicycle Corps."

Lieutenant Moss might have slipped into obscurity with his wacky idea, were it not for a sympathetic ear: Lieutenant General Nelson A. Miles, who was equally enchanted by the martial possibilities of the bicycle. General Miles composed a report in 1895, stating, "The bicycle has been found exceedingly useful in reconnoitering different sections of the country." He was eager for a demonstration.

Lieutenant Moss was stationed in Missoula, Montana, a town of 40,000 that was fairly close to the middle of nowhere. But the 25th Infantry wasn't just any regiment; all the enlistees were African-American. In Western lore—and Reggae songs—the segregated company was known as the Buffalo Soldiers. And under the leadership of Lieutenant Moss, they would road-test a new kind of war machine.

First, Moss received a shipment of bicycles from Spalding, the sporting goods company that still makes basketballs and volleyball nets today. The bikes had state-of-the-art steel rims, which were much better than the usual wooden wheels. But there was only one gear; once a hill got too steep, soldiers had to dismount and push their vehicles up the inclines. Fully loaded with personal effects, each bike could weigh as much as 70 pounds.

Moss arranged daily rides with his troops. He led a nine-man trip to Yellowstone, several hundred miles away, then several hundred miles back. The going was tough, but the route was successful.

At last, Moss organized his dream expedition: 1,900 miles from Fort Missoula to St. Louis, Missouri. Twenty men mounted their Spalding bikes on June 14, 1897, including a physician and newspaper reporter. They journeyed for six weeks, cutting across the frontier on wagon trails and railroad beds. They slogged through rainstorms and fixed many flats. Much of the land was still wilderness, devoid of pavement or dependable bridges. But they succeeded in their mission; the Buffalo Soldiers coasted into St. Louis on July 24, along with nearly 1,000 cyclists who had followed their progress in the papers.

Lieutenant Moss didn't waste any time. He proposed a follow-up ride, this one to California. But General Miles declined. Moss had proven his point, and one experiment felt like enough. With that, the bicycle faded from U.S. military history, more or less forever.

The Cons

The tactical benefits of a bicycle are obvious, especially in a steam-powered epoch. But so are the drawbacks.

Obviously, you can't fight while riding a bike. The recoil from the smallest pistol would knock a man off-balance. Cyclists ride high and concentrate on the road, so they're sitting ducks for marksmen. The only real advantage is transport, and by the onset of World War I, trucks and tanks had made them obsolete. Only 17 years after the Buffalo Soldiers made their landmark journey, the entire nature of war had changed. Automobiles, motorcycles, airplanes, and troop carriers were all perfected within those two decades. The idea of a bicycle corps suddenly looked ridiculous. This exciting new technology had barely taken the stage before it got the hook.

Bikes have still played a role in wartime events, but in sneakier ways. Bike messengers have peppered the battlefield, as have bike-borne spies. During World War II, the Italian racer Gino Bartali famously stored secret messages in his frame to undermine the Fascist regime. After the Invasion of Normandy, Ernest Hemingway rode a bicycle from one battlefront to another to report on the Allied advance. During the Vietnam War, covert assassins—many of them women and children—would hurl grenades into groups of U.S. marines. Then they'd ride away, blending into the crowds of civilian cyclists, as the bombs exploded behind them. None of these are standard procedure for a standing army.

But one idea persists, intriguing generals to this day. If a bicycle is best for subterfuge—and for quick, individual movements—could it still be useful to a paratrooper? During a drop, paratroopers can be carried on the wind and scattered all over enemy lines. Their toughest challenge is to regroup, often at night and in varied terrain, without getting spotted by the enemy. Could bicycles help them on their mission?

Somebody thought so. The Birmingham Small Arms Company assembled more than 60,000 such bikes for the British military during World War II. They were deployed all across the European front, from France to Norway.

These were folding bikes, a novel idea at the time, which paratroopers could carry on their descents. Most of these bikes were abandoned in the field or scooped up by locals. But by gum, they did their duty.

Making the Leap

Half a century later, Montague revisited the same concept.

The Montague headquarters are in Somerville, Massachusetts, where the company was founded in 1987. For me, a digital window shopper, this was part of the company's appeal; Somerville is just ninety minutes north of my house in Rhode Island. The founder, David Montague, graduated from the Massachusetts Institute of Technology. In my mind, a Montague bike would qualify as "buying local."

The company was ten years old when it won a two-year development grant from the Defense Advanced Research Projects Agency. What DARPA wanted was a folding bike, possibly equipped with an electric motor.

Just when you think there's no new way to fold a bike, Montague devised a new method. The front wheel comes completely off; the pivot point isn't in the middle of the top tube—as it is for most folding bikes—but farther back, just beneath the seat post. Layered together, the folded pieces look less like a triangle than a square. For later models, Montague added a bike rack, which flips around and serves as a stabilizer; no kickstand required. Sleek aluminum gives the Paratrooper a commanding presence, especially when painted forest green.

Like the Hummer, the Paratrooper has become a commercial vehicle, available to anyone with a thousand dollars and love for mountain bikes. Actually, Montague put out a line of Paratroopers specifically designed to fit into Hummers. Today, Montague sells a fleet of different models, from urban commuters to all-terrain e-bikes.

As far as I know, the Paratrooper never served in actual combat. They were used in at least one simulation, where soldier-cyclists successfully "rescued" a group of "hostages" from their "captors." It's hard to imagine bikes being dropped into Baghdad or Kandahar, or platoons of paratroopers securing a village on slick MTBs. A soldier isn't a bicycle cop, and guerilla fighters aren't muggers. But as late as 1999, the Department of Defense was still investing in the possibility. The siren song of a battle-ready bicycle is difficult to ignore.

Give Peace a Chance

Call me sentimental, but I'm glad bicycles never took off as war machines. This one invention has transformed civilization in so many ways, and we're still finding new applications in our 21st century lives. But if this elegant arrangement of gears and wheels has to fall short somewhere, let it be in the business of fighting people.

I like to think the armed services have plenty of toys to play with, from drones and cluster bombs to submarines and nuclear missiles. Lots of good has come out of government R&D: household items like duct tape and EpiPens were birthed in the military-industrial complex. Just about every patent, no matter how benign, has crossed a general's desk, bringing with it the unfortunate question: *How can we weaponize this?*

But bicycles never really made the cut. They're peaceful by nature, a toy for children and a panacea for adults. Time in the saddle keeps most of us happy and healthy. Bicycles connect us, across neighborhoods and nations. Millions of people make a living by riding them. They're built for peace. And for someone like me, that's valorous enough.

If a Tree Falls in the Woods

A FALLEN TREE blocks the path. This is no surprise; after a windy storm, the Washington Secondary Bike Trail is usually strewn with debris.

But this is a *whole tree.* The foliage is voluminous and green. The trunk still looks healthy—except that it's horizontal, barricading the whole trail.

Well, not the *whole* trail. Recent travelers have blazed a little track on one side. If you pedal carefully, you can slip between the fallen tree and the woods. Which is exactly what I did a half-hour earlier.

Now I'm returning in the opposite direction. A simple there-and-back. Twenty miles in total. The trail that was previously a gradual climb is now a refreshing descent. Gravity guides me down the asphalt, and I coast toward the tree. The pavement along this stretch is ribbed with roots, but otherwise it's blissful riding.

A second cyclist flies past me. He wears a Lycra suit and he leans into his drop-bars. Again, perfectly normal; the Washington Secondary is less trafficked than other Rhode

Island trails, so it's not bad for race training. I say hello. The racer nods back. And that's the last I expect to see of him before he careens around the bend and disappears forever.

I round the tree. For a split second, I plan to continue. But then I see the racer—the same cyclist who just passed me. He's stopped. He's standing next to his bike, looking back on the trail he's just covered.

"Hey, man," he calls. "Are you okay?"

My brakes squeal. I look at the racer, confused. Then I follow his gaze—to the tree.

A human shape emerges. Beneath the layers of branches and leaves. The figure is hard to make out; he's dressed in black jeans and a black T-shirt. His skin is pale and his arms skinny. His mouth has traces of facial hair. He's young, probably a teenager. His limbs are tangled around a bicycle— not a hybrid, like mine, or a racing bike, like the other guy's, but a little BMX bike, the kind you see doing tricks at your local skatepark.

"I didn't even see it," the kid moans. "I didn't even know a tree was there. I was just going, and—and I tried to stop, but I just..."

A minute later, we know everything. The kid was headed to Warwick Mall, where he works at a restaurant. He bombed down the hill, just like he always does, and the tree appeared out of nowhere. BMX bikes aren't known for their brakes. He tried to stop, then swerve, but it was too late. His front wheel struck wood, and bike and body flew into the branches.

"My leg hurts," he groans.

"How bad is it?" I ask, wondering whether we should try to move him. "Does it feel broken?"

"Nah," he says. "I think it's just sprained."

"Okay," I say. "Gimme your hands."

Carefully, I pull the kid out of the tree. He leans into his good foot; I let him throw an arm over my shoulders. He hops forward, onto clear pavement, where he finds a place to sit down and nurse his leg. The racer grabs the kid's bike and backpack. The kid takes deep breaths; his grin is a mix of relief and embarrassment. After all, he's been ambushed by nothing more hostile than a dead maple.

"There's a road at the bottom of the hill," I say, realizing he probably knew that already. "Do you have Uber on your phone? Lyft?"

The kid shakes his head. "But my buddy can pick me up. I'll just tell him where I'm at."

When we're convinced the kid is okay, the racer and I bike away. I'm glad the racer stopped; I don't know if I would have heard the kid through the din of my daydreams. As we pedal away, the racer grimaces. "Poor kid," he says, and speeds beyond sight.

Headers

For the last seven miles, I think about what I've just seen. An accident. A bike accident. A bike accident that didn't involve a car. And it dawns on me just how long it's been since I've seen one like this. I wonder, in fact, how many such accidents I've even seen in my life.

Actually, I *do* remember the last bike accident I saw: it was maybe ten years ago, in the small town of St. Marys, Pennsylvania. It was a muggy summer day, and I was taking a walk through St. Marys' business district. As I turned onto a side-street, I saw a man lying on the sidewalk.

The man was athletic-looking, probably in his thirties. He wore a Spandex suit. A nice touring bike lay next to him. His body was limp, twisted in the unnatural way of someone who's been suddenly knocked unconscious. There was no blood, no skid mark, no broken glass. The guy was just lying there, as still as a corpse.

I whipped out my phone and called 911.

A minute later, the man stirred. Other pedestrians appeared, and they knelt down, asking if he was okay. Sirens sounded in the distance.

And that was it. I never found out who the cyclist was, how he'd crashed, the extent of his injuries. In the years since, I more or less forgot about it.

The truth is, we cyclists *can* get hurt, all on our own. We can take a turn too fast. Our tires can burst in the middle of a steep hill. We can trip over gutters, get shrubbery stuck in our spokes, hit our heads on low-hanging objects. We are fully capable of breaking femurs, giving ourselves concussions, or—heaven forbid—hitting pedestrians.

Once, while I was pedaling through a rain-drenched forest in Connecticut, a dead bough broke off a tree. It crashed to the ground, about thirty feet in front of me. I wove around the shattered pieces and persisted down the trail. But for days, I thought about that near-miss. What if I'd been riding just a little faster? Sometimes, the Butterfly Effect lets you off the hook.

Other times, you crash your BMX bike into a fallen tree and injure your knee-cap. But if you cycle regularly, you know where I'm going with this. You know how unlikely it is that you'll just slam your bike into a wall. You know how mild these dust-ups usually are. You won't be surprised that, out of the 1,089 people who died bicycling in 2019, 83 percent of them collided with motor vehicles.

To be fair, that does mean that 377 cyclists died in other ways. Maybe they were reckless. Maybe they succumbed to dehydration, or stroke, or "acts of God." Maybe some were mountain bikers who suffered a bad landing. A death is tragic, no matter how it comes to pass.

I could go on and on about how much I personally hate driving, how much I resent cars on the road, how much I wish the U.S. had more dedicated bike lanes—and, like, *actual* bike lanes, not just faded stripes of paint. Nothing gets my hackles up like one particular road sign, about the size of a manila envelope: "Share the Road!" As if motorists could possibly give a shit. Cyclists are always at odds with cars, and vice versa. When I get behind the wheel—almost every day—I feel sick with self-loathing. I'm operating the same machine that I spend so much of my life fearing. Give me a beer or two, and I'll never shut up about it.

But I have to stop myself. Because on that one afternoon, the accident was benign. There were no cars. There was no perpetrator. The crash took place on a bike trail—the flattest, emptiest surface there is. The kid should have looked where he was going, but really, who expects a tree? And in the end, he was fine. Bruised, humiliated, maybe late for work. But fine.

I can never be reminded too much that everyone makes mistakes. And one day, when I hit a chasmic pothole and fly over my handlebars, I'll remember that kid on the Washington Secondary Bike Trail. I'll remember him and think, "Well, it happens."

Paved with Good Intentions

I'm RIDING DOWN the Trunkline Trail. My Trek hybrid hobbles over pebbles and roots. The forest is a deep green— it's September, and the air is cool, but it doesn't yet feel like fall. The path dips down, out of the woods, and I cross a country road.

And then I stop. The trail continues on the other side, but there's something in the way. A chain-link fence. The gate hangs slightly open. There's plenty of room to slip through. But I also see a sign, printed in deadly red letters against a white background: DANGER: DO NOT ENTER.

I look around. The road is empty, even of cars. A farmhouse stands nearby, and cows graze in a pasture. But there's no one to ask. All I have are a few physical clues— and my own finicky judgment.

My first instinct is to go around. "Danger" is danger, no matter how ambiguous. I look at Google Maps, and if I ride a few miles out of my way, I'll end up at the same intersection.

And yet—I can clearly see a single-track path, sliced into

thick grass. My paper map illustrates an unbroken route from Franklin, Massachusetts, to Wallum Pond. Google Maps shows a faded green line, and if I follow this line, I will arrive at the next segment in one direct mile.

And, like, *the gate is open.*

I imagine all the things that could go wrong. Will an animal trap clamp over my wheel? Will a gas line explode? Will a man appear, dressed in Carhartt's and cradling a shotgun, as he growls, *I reckon you made a wrong turn, city boy...*

I weigh the pros and cons. I take a swig of water. I consider how long this detour could take, and how lost I could get, and how pointless that might be.

And then, before I even realize what I'm doing, I roll forward, through the gate, and down the forbidden path.

The Road Less Traveled

On paper, the Southern New England Trunkline Trail is a former railroad line that runs for 22 miles along the Rhode Island-Massachusetts border. You start in Franklin State Forest, and you end up in Douglas State Forest. If you live a good deal south, these names don't mean much; the whole region is rural and wooded, with a few old mill towns scattered between. Unless you know the area, or you keep looking at your digital map, you never really know what town you've entered, or even which state you're standing in.

On local signs, the Trunkline Trail goes by the acronym "SNETT." On the Franklin side, there's a sizable parking lot, and I'm welcomed with a big sign and a rack of physical maps. For the first few miles, I pedal blithely down a wide gravel trail. I dip into a few shallow craters, carved over time by mud puddles. The forest is dark and beautiful.

But like a lot of rail-trail systems, SNETT isn't so much a single path as a patchwork of different paths.

Like, *very* different paths. Gravel turns into smooth pavement. Smooth pavement turns into sandy dirt. Sandy dirt turns into a rocky corridor with earthen bumps and ramps, clearly designed for mountain bikes. Then, for 3.5 miles, the SNETT becomes the Blackstone River Greenway, a ribbon of blacktop so pristine you could eat off it.

And beyond the Greenway? The SNETT theoretically continues for another 10 miles, but information about this half of the trail is almost impossible to find. Which is why I'm riding the SNETT today.

But then there's this sign, warning me about some anonymous "danger." The words say *stop.* The unlocked gate says *keep going.*

This isn't the first time I've gotten mixed messages to-day. A few miles earlier, the trail stopped at another country road. Some locals were chatting at the trailhead, and I asked how to keep going.

"Oh, wow, I'm not sure," said one.

"I think it picks up behind the police station," said the other. "But that's about five miles away."

"They're supposed to connect them," offered the first.

"That's what they say. But I don't know how you're supposed to get there now."

I thanked them and moved on. About one minute later, I spotted a little hand-painted sign that said, "SNETT," and pointed down an innocuous road. I pedaled a short way and found another trailhead. Mostly, I was relieved, but I had to wonder: *How is it people who live here—who are actively using this path—don't know where it goes?*

I hate to say it, but I think part of the reason is, simply: New England.

Slow Your Roll

A few months ago, I had this harebrained idea to bike the Bay Circuit Trail, a 200-mile crescent through Boston's metro area. The route is magnificent, connecting such famous landmarks as Walden Pond and Plymouth Bay. This sounded like a perfect weeklong road-trip—and so close to my home in Rhode Island that it practically qualified as a "staycation."

But as I started my research, I read this deal-breaking paragraph: "The Bay Circuit is open to hiking, trail running and picnicking, and in the winter, snowshoeing. Certain parts of the trail are suitable for bicycling..."

Certain parts. Not the whole thing. At some point, you have to stop cycling, find your way to a regular road, and pray you can find the next bikeable part.

Because the "circuit" isn't one continuous, linear park controlled by a single entity, but "a coalition of state, town, and federal agencies, non-profit organizations, and individuals." Every few miles, the management changes, and so do the rules. And you don't really know what you're dealing with until you get there.

Let me be clear: I *love* that these trails exist, period. And for the vast majority of people, they work just fine. Want to take a quick promenade? Walk the dog? Day-hike? Out-and-back? Great. Pick any segment, and you'll have a great time. Fresh air. Wildlife. A symphony of birdsong. The whole bit.

But it's very different for people like me, who want to start at "the beginning" and bike to "the end." When it comes to the SNETT, this 22-mile trail feels messy, unpredictable, a work in progress. Sometimes there are signs and mile posts; other times there aren't. Some sections are so swampy and rugged that the only way to ride confidently would be on a fat tire bike with ample suspension. And there's no way to tell, from any map or website, that this is what you're up against.

Again, I'm not complaining. I wanted an adventure, and I got it. And these conditions only make sense: the Puritans conquered these lands nearly 400 years ago, and the early colonists frantically claimed every acre they could. The terrain was rocky and blanketed in forest. Most people got around on foot, and Colonial roads weren't much more refined than these gravel paths. It's not just Massachusetts; much of the eastern seaboard is similarly splintered, where tiny parcels of public and private land confusingly overlap. There's a lot of history here, including the rise and fall of whole railroad lines, and as a visitor, it's impossible to tell who's in charge of what.

So it might be a little frustrating, for a tiny minority of cross-country cyclists. But I understand. It takes a village to build a bike trail; and sometimes, it takes a whole coalition of villages.

That said, I still have no idea whether I'm trespassing on this land.

I pedal my way down the single track. I see a pond, some houses, until it all becomes forest. A blue jay flitters from branch to branch. Crickets hum in the underbrush.

Except for the tread marks printed in the soil, I can't see a trace of human life.

In my mind, I rehearse what I will say if someone appears. *Oh, did the sign say 'danger'? I must have missed it!* Or: *I thought 'do not enter' just referred to cars.* Or: *I'm so glad you're here! Any idea which way to Worcester?*

But no one does. A mile later, I reach the end of the trail. I see houses ahead, with sloped roofs and freshly mown lawns. I also see a gate, along with two signs: PRIVATE PROPERTY: NO TRESPASSING. And: WALKING DOGS PROHIBITED.

Once again, I have no idea what to make of this. I have no dog. But if I cross this gate, will someone call the cops? Is this part of the trail? Is there a special arrangement? And if so, why doesn't it say so? Somewhere? *Anywhere?*

I press ahead. But because the grass is so well maintained, I heave my bike onto my shoulder and carry it to the curb. If I get arrested, the least I can do is deny messing up their turf.

Give a Hoot?

The rest of my ride passes without incident. I hit the Greenway, and dozens of cyclists trickle past me, nodding and mumbling, "Mahnin." (I can never get enough of the Eastern Massachusetts accent).

Eventually, the trail is too muddy to continue. I turn around and head back the way I came, satisfied with a 23-mile jaunt in a place I've never been.

I pass through the same residential development, and I find the same single-track. From this direction, there is no "danger" sign at all.

Halfway down, I spot hikers. A man and woman with silvery hair. They smile and wave.

I can't help myself; I put on the brakes.

"Could you tell me if this land is private?" I say.

The couple trades glances. They have no idea what I could mean by this.

"There's a sign, up ahead. Says, 'danger, do not enter'? I just want to make sure I'm not trespassing."

The man nods. "Ah, well all this used to belong to the railroad. If that's what you mean by private."

"Sometimes kids would drive through on their dirt bikes," added the woman, "and they probably don't want anyone like *that* around here. But as for you and me? They probably couldn't give a hoot." She laughs off the idea.

I thank them. We all smile and go our separate ways.

And there I have it: no one could give a hoot.

All I had to do was ask.

THE PERSPIRATION PARADOX

IN RHODE ISLAND, seven miles is a long way. Not just because the state is small—it is, obviously—but because the landscape changes so radically. When I fasten my bike helmet, I'm standing in front of my house on a residential street.

A few blocks later, I'm pedaling through commercial sprawl...

...I cut through a school campus and an athletic park...

...I hit the rail-trail, and I coast through the woods for a good mile or so...

...the trail ends, and I navigate a congested highway underpass...

...I weave through deadlock traffic on a narrow street in a dense neighborhood, where the cars are rusty and reckless and pedestrians hurl themselves in front of them...

...eventually I take a bridge over Interstate 95, and eight lanes of morning rush hour roar beneath me...

...I cut through the high-rises and office towers of Downcity...

...I cross a stone bridge over the Providence River...

...I skirt the waterfront green space of India Point Park...

...a bike path takes me along the Seekonk River...

...I emerge among the boutiques and cafes of Wayland Square, the most fashionable neighborhood in Providence...

...I ride a long, tree-lined street, until I come to a cluster of stately buildings. I lock my bike outside.

I feel amazing. I've beaten traffic. I've given off zero emissions. I'm energized and ready for the day.

And also—I am *drenched* in sweat. My shirt is soaked though. My eyes sting. My hair is several shades darker and furrowed from my bike helmet. I can barely peel off my fingerless gloves. My deodorant is failing me on every level.

I need a shower, stat.

And luckily—incredibly—I can use one, and change my outfit, in the 15 minutes before I start my shift.

Everything Works on Paper

"What are you reading?" asked my wife the other night, as we settled into bed.

I turned the book cover toward her. It was a peppy orange paperback with the self-explanatory title, *How Cycling Can Save the World.*

"Oh," said K., who is accustomed to my obsession. "How is it?"

I smirked. "It's about three hundred pages of confirmation bias. And I'm *loving* it."

Truly, this has been one of my favorite books of the year. The author, Peter Walker, is a British journalist who usually writes about politics for *The Guardian*. But he's also a diehard cyclist. Walker spent much of his childhood as a self-doubting asthmatic; then he started working as a bike courier in the unforgiving streets of London, and he steadily transformed. The bicycle empowered him; it rescued him from physical—and psychological—inertia. Walker wants cycling to become a practical mode of transport, and he truly believes his titular claim, that cycling can "save the world."

Walker uses hundreds of examples, mostly from Denmark and the Netherlands, where widespread cycling has radically improved the quality of life. To an American cyclist living in the suburbs, Walker's descriptions of bike-centric urban planning are pretty much pornographic. Walker backs every idea with studies and statistics. He returns to the same thesis over and over, that practical cycling is just common sense, and society should do everything in its power to promote it.

As he writes in his introduction:

> *"If cycling is going to indeed change the world, it won't be the Lycra-clad road warriors who'll be doing it. The big changes — and they can be huge — happen when a nation doesn't see cycling as a hobby, a sport, a mission, let alone a way of life. They happen when it becomes nothing more than a convenient, quick, cheap way of getting about, with the unintended bonus being the fact that you get some exercise in the process."*

Yes, I thought. *Deal me in.* I tore through the book in record time. I fully embraced Walker's two-wheeled vision of

the future. I was the choir, and Walker was preaching directly to me. If I could have woken up in Walker's world of
never-ending bike-lanes and motorless grocery trips, I would
have.

Except—one thing was missing. One small but significant
detail. In all his research and data points, all his personal
anecdotes and myriad interviews with experts, Walker barely
mentions the problem that millions of bike-commuters
would face: what about sweat?

Pardon My Glands

Let me be frank: I sweat *a lot*. Once the temperature hits 75,
I start to glisten. Five degrees more, and my face is dripping.
By 85 degrees, my T-shirt is damp and I can barely turn a
door handle. At 90, my pores are basically faucets.

This often works to my advantage. I love a warm summer day, and the slightest breeze cools me down. But let's
just say that perspiration is not my most attractive feature.
I've lived most of my life in humid places, where it's perfectly normal to change my outfit two or three times a day. I've
never overheated, even in the height of an Arizona summer,
when the mercury hits 120 degrees. Believe me, though—it
ain't pretty.

Why should you have to know anything about my pro-
lific epithelial glands? Only this: I'm a fit, motivated cyclist. I
don't get to commute by bike often—only a few times per
month—but I *would* do it every day if I could. I know my
somewhat complicated route to work; I have several decent
bikes; and I've navigated urban traffic for years. My work-
place has not one but *two* bike racks outside. Even my em-

ployers encourage my rides. The circumstances are nearly perfect.

Except that, after seven miles, I show up looking like a drowned cat.

Why does this ride still work? Because there are showers in my building. Actually, there's an entire gym in my building. One of my employee benefits is that I can use these facilities for free.

Here is the problem with Walker's Utopia: riding a bike can be messy business. Summers tend to be hot, no matter where you live. Most places have regular rainstorms. Cities are built on every kind of terrain, and some are hilly or even mountainous. Even in a hypothetical city where combustion engines are outlawed, people will show up at work looking (and smelling) awful. I love watching videos of perfectly quaffed businessmen zipping through European capitals on their one-speed bikes, but that's just the magic of advertising.

In reality, one heat wave will make them look like hurricane survivors. And that's just *men* in business attire; never mind the aesthetic demands made on professional women.

I've been in the workforce for a quarter-century, and only this most recent job has provided on-site showers. Still, I've commuted by bike with alarming regularity. I rode six miles to a restaurant to wait tables. I rode three miles (and then took a thirty-minute bus ride) for a data-entry job. I rode five miles to teach classes at a university. I rode seven miles to do copywriting for a website. I rode eight miles to help edit a magazine. None of these jobs were based in Utrecht or Copenhagen, where bike commutes are perfectly routine. I had to carry extra clothes, change in bathroom stalls, pat my face with paper towels, and cake my body in antiperspirant—all the while feeling sticky and pungent. A five-minute rinse would have made all the difference.

A lack of showers isn't a dealbreaker. I realize that many people live in flat cities, and so ask less of their bodies. Millions live only a couple miles from their work. Not every job requires collared shirts and khakis. Only a fraction—like me—have young children they have to personally take to school and then pick up at the end of the day. People don't sweat much in spring and autumn, which make up half the year in temperate climates. Throw some ebikes into the mix, and bike commuting sounds downright pleasant.

But I'm skeptical. Americans like to be comfortable. We love air conditioning and drive-thru coffee. Above all, we like to be clean—and groomed, and conditioned, and ex-foliated—at all times. If an American climbs a stairwell to reach the fourth floor, he might as well be Amish. We'll on-ly tolerate sweat at the gym, as long as we use alcohol wipes to disinfect every single thing we've touched. Short of a zombie apocalypse, that cultural norm won't change over-night. Or even in a generation.

One option is to normalize showers at work. That's a pretty wacky idea, of course. The U.S. has taken decades just to install ramps and automatic doors to earn ADA ap-proval; no business will voluntarily rip up its own bathrooms and add shower stalls just to appease a few health nuts. There's also the environmental impact: commuters with showers might double their water use—an insane proposition in draught-stricken places like California and the Southwest.

A better option is the good old-fashioned "duck bath." The moment you've locked your bike, you beeline for the restroom, change into work clothes, and scrub yourself down with scented towelettes. It's not ideal, and you'll probably throw *something* in the trash, but at least you won't have wasted 17 gallons of fresh water. This is a practice familiar to millions of people in China, where professional appearance is important but personal resources are thin—and cycling to work, of course, is absolutely normal.

Personally, I'm fine with duck baths, as long as the restroom is sizable and clean. But I also don't put much effort into my appearance. I don't worry about my $20 hairstyle from Supercuts. I can stomach a few wrinkles in my dress shirts from Target. I wear the same pair of shoes for all but the most formal occasions. You can't expect a hotel concierge or trial lawyer to be so carefree.

I would love to be wrong about all this. Maybe we're all more adaptable than I realize. If humanity could adapt to masks and Purell stations, could we also accept shiny faces and gamy smells, if only out of necessity? Could we come to ignore all the pit stains and mussed hair? Without question, I still want to wake up and live in that world, no matter how many outfits I have to carry. My only question is—will anyone else?

All Aboard!

I'm standing on a railroad platform, and I'm about to do something I've wanted to do for years.

It's nothing crazy. It may be the simplest thing you can do while standing up.

With one hand, I clutch my handlebars. With the other, I hold my saddle to steady the bike. My Dahon Curl is heavy—weighed down by loaded panniers, a four-season sleeping bag, and a tent. I push forward, through the door, and into a waiting train.

And that's it. *That's* what I've waited much of my adult life to do: put my bike on a train.

Even now, as I steady my Dahon against the wall and push down a retractable seat, I feel like I'm getting away with a crime. Even though the online schedule says "bikes permitted." Even though there's a bicycle graphic printed on the side of this passenger car. Even though there's a rack built into the wall so you can safely fasten your bike with two rubber straps. *It still feels too good to be true.*

The train is practically empty. It's 11 a.m., after all. I ask a conductor where, exactly, I can put my bike. I explain that I've never done this before.

"Anywhere you like," he says, and strides into the next car. He barely even looks at my digital ticket.

Derailed

I love trains. But it's more than that: I have *always* loved trains. I love to watch a locomotive storm across the countryside. I'm comforted by the sight of steel rails, even defunct ones. And nothing soothes me in the middle of the night like the moan of a distant air horn and rumble that follows.

As a kid, I played with model trains, running Märklin tracks across our living room floor. I also collected model kits, building HO-scale houses and shops. My villages were populated by inch-tall plastic citizens, who ran errands on Main Street, then rode my trains across the carpet. I decorated the landscape with miniature trees and bushes made from actual lichen. None of this was impressive; adult hobbyists can be downright fanatical. My efforts were cute by comparison, but man, did I love it.

Maybe I should have grown up in Western Europe, where trains run everywhere. Or maybe I should have grown up in the early 20th Century, in the heyday of the American railroad. But I didn't. I'm a Gen-X American, and I have no idea what it's like to see my entire society connected by rails.

When the Interstate Highway System took hold in the 1950s, millions of passengers flocked to car dealerships. Ticket sales plummeted, as did the number of functioning lines. Within twenty years, the American railroad system nearly collapsed. In a last-ditch effort to save mass transit, the Nixon Administration (of all administrations) passed the Rail Passenger Service Act in 1971. The result was Amtrak—that anemic, "quasi-public corporation," with its outdated engines and impressive delays, which we have all been forced to accept as our national rail service.

Amtrak isn't alone, of course. Commuter trains exist in cities across the country, from the Bay Area Rapid Transit (BART) to the Long Island Railroad (LIRR), with a variety of networks in between.

But as much as I've moved around, I've never lived in a place where trains were useful. I never resided near a station. Or if I did, the train didn't go where I needed to be. Even if it did, I'd probably have to drive to the station, which meant parking, which meant *paying* for parking.

Which is why, in most of my past neighborhoods, rail service was kind of a novelty act. In Pittsburgh, the light rail goes only from Downtown to the South Hills; it doesn't even connect to the airport. In Phoenix, the light rail snakes through multiple cities, but the developments are so spread out, I might still have to take an Uber from the light rail platform to a specific address. In Boston, I simply lived too far from Forest Hills station; just getting there in morning rush hour (by bus or car) could take 45 minutes, and *then* I had to wait for the actual train.

Hopping Trains

But there's always the bicycle.

I have long fantasized about this idea—of pedaling my bike from house to station; rolling the bike onto a passenger car; then riding the train to some distant place. No traffic; no need to pay for gas. No fight for parking spaces. No meter maids. No fender-benders. No need to even think.

And I'm not alone. This is the progressive urban planner's favorite daydream: a mixed-use development, full of municipal green space, standing only a few blocks away from a light-rail platform. In architectural mock-ups, it's not so much a suburb as an "integrated, medium-density, residential community." And everywhere you look, there's bicycle infrastructure: lanes, paths, and racks, freshly built for the urban commuter.

But I also know I'm in the minority. Americans love to drive. They cling to the privacy of their cars, and they recoil at the idea of sharing space with other people. (COVID, understandably, has only worsened this misanthropy.) They don't care how well this system works in Japan. They don't want to hear how great it is for the environment. They don't even want to know how much money they'll save. For most Americans, the idea of cycling to work, much less putting a bike on a train, is ostentatiously weird. They can't even imagine what that lifestyle would look like.

Love Train

So today, I sit on the MBTA commuter train, and I count myself lucky. It's taken me four decades to live in a place where this ride is possible—to simply board a train with my bike and ride to another city. And even after I moved here, it took three years to find the right occasion to actually take this trip.

I hunker down in my seat. I feel the train pull out of the station. Through the wide window, suburban Providence scrolls past—warehouses and cement walls and triple-decker houses.

I'm euphoric. In my saddlebags, I have everything I need for a multi-day trip. I'll stay in Boston, catch up with friends, and stow my folding bike in my hotel room. Then I'll ride over to the seaport and take the ferry to Provincetown. Nowhere on this journey is a car required, not even a taxi.

For a few minutes, the train rides parallel to I-95, and I watch cars fly down their lines. I've driven that route hundreds of times, back when I used to commute between Boston and Pawtucket. In a word, it was horrible: gridlock and construction and crazy drivers and every kind of bad weather. There was nothing to look at, just an endless queue of trees and trucks. And yet, I had to pay fervent attention, every second, to prevent my Yaris from colliding into something at 75 miles per hour.

Now, on the train, all I have to do is stare out the window and listen to a Pandora playlist. I lazily check my email. I watch the blur of forest and small towns. I nod off a little. It's bliss.

The hour passes like a dream. I know that isn't always the case; boarding the train in the late morning is the best of circumstances, when rush hour is long over. Still, I savor every second. I feel like I have the whole train to myself. And when the train pulls into Ruggles Station, I rise from my seat, grasp my handlebars, and guide my bike through the open door.

I have arrived. Refreshed. And ready.

Ghost Bike

Nine years, I think, pedaling a borrowed bicycle down Braddock Avenue, *and so much is the same.*

I coast past familiar storefronts—a café, an indie cinema, a mural of birds in flight. Traffic flows around me, leaving a narrow space between moving cars and parked ones. The lawns and trees are exactly as I remember them. My heart throbs, not with exertion, but with love.

"Feel free to take it all day," said my friend Bill, who's hosting me in his spare room and loaned me this bike. He said this during our long night of Yeunglings and pool at the local bar. "I'll text you after work and see where you are."

Even the generosity is the same.

Really, it's only been three years since I last visited Pittsburgh, and I would've been here sooner, if not for COVID-19. But scattered drop-ins are nothing like living here. A decade ago, my wife and I owned a condo in Point Breeze, and that was a good time in our life. I miss so many things, but *this* in particular: cruising around on a wonky bicycle. Soon, I'm flying down my old street, between rows of suburban lots, past the iron gates of my old complex, which looks exactly as I left it.

Today I will ride twenty-seven miles around the city, from the eastern edge of Regent Square to a warehouse district beyond the West End Bridge—basically, across city limits and back. My reunion must be thorough, physical, full-contact. I will explore this city the way I did when I lived here: on two wheels, propelled by my own two legs. My tire will skirt all Three Rivers. I'll cut through about sixteen distinct neighborhoods, which I could once fluently navigate. I'll climb nearly 1,000 feet, much of it potholed or paved with cobblestone. The weather is spring-cool. The sky is a merciful blend of clouds and sun. I will treasure every block, because it really has been too long.

But when I arrive in the busy hub of South Oakland, something will happen. Sweat-soaked and achy, I will heave my bike up a long, concrete staircase and emerge from the woods behind the Frick Fine Arts Center. I'll pedal into traffic, making a slow circle around the greensward of Schenley Plaza. And there, beneath the thirty-six-story gothic stonework of the Cathedral of Learning, I'll see it: the Ghost Bike.

The bike, painted white and locked to a steel post, will stand silently on the sidewalk, a memorial to the woman who lost her life here.

And in that moment, I'll take stock of everything that's different. Because it's *not* the same Pittsburgh I remember—and I don't mean new high-rises, shuttered businesses, or graying friends. For a cyclist who's been away for a while, the city exhibits radical transformation. Spotting that Ghost Bike will fill me with anger and heartache. I will wish, for the thousandth time, that this memorial didn't have to exist. But

I will also marvel at all the change that began with a single accident. And I will wonder what Susan would think of it all.

Who She Was

I can't exaggerate: Susan Hicks really was one of the kindest and most genuine people I ever met. She really did love to smile, and to laugh, and did both all the time. But the way I remember her is consistently *chill*. Everything she did looked effortless and easygoing, as if she'd just woken up from an afternoon nap. She had straight blond hair and sleepy eyes; her cadence reminded me of snowboarders. Everyone loved her.

Susan and I weren't bosom buddies; there were legions of people who knew her better. But we ran into each other again and again, usually at house parties, for years. My memories are hazy, but some stand out: talking together about theater for a solid hour on the fire escape of somebody's apartment. Rolling sushi on a butcher block in somebody's kitchen. And yes, once riding bikes around Schenley Park with a posse of friends. Throughout our twenties, Pittsburgh was busy with rooftop shindigs, ersatz music events, and gallery openings. Susan and I were always bumping into each other, and I was always pleased as punch to see her.

Like so many of those friends, Susan was dynamic and whip-smart. A Virginia native, Susan had lived in Russia, Serbia, and Puerto Rico. She earned a PhD in anthropology from the University of British Columbia. By her mid-thirties, Susan was assistant director of academic affairs at the Center for Russian and East European Studies, a showcase program at the University of Pittsburgh. She joined a rowing team.

She was fluent in the Russian language. She organized regular get-togethers with friends, when they would divvy up roles and read Shakespeare aloud. If anyone deserved to live a long and happy life, it was Susan.

A Hole in the World

I learned about the accident on my twenty-sixth birthday. My Facebook account was littered with posts—alerts, exclamations, updates, and so many woeful comments, a new one every few minutes. If social media could wail in anguish, it wailed that day.

The facts emerged: Susan was riding her bike down Forbes Avenue, a major artery in Pittsburgh. She routinely commuted to work, and Forbes was one of her regular routes. Out of nowhere, a car collided with her bike; she was "pinned," according to reports, an image I refuse to let myself imagine. Susan was critically injured. She was rushed to a hospital, but it was too late to save her.

The driver, it turned out, was high on some kind of "synthetic marijuana." He didn't have a license. When police arrived, he allegedly "faked a seizure." In press photos, the man is unkempt, his expression inscrutably grim. His face contrasts sharply with Susan's beaming portrait. But there they were, paired together on the evening news, killer and victim, forever bound in each other's tragic story. That face would reappear six months later, when the driver was arrested, and again in 2017, when he was sentenced to five-and-a-half to nine years in prison for involuntary manslaughter.

"Death of cyclist, Pitt educator leaves hole in community," read a headline in the *Pittsburgh Tribune Review.*

A hole, yes. There was no better word for it.

Reality Check

The accident proved something that everyone knew, but no City Council had ever really addressed: Pittsburgh was a deadly place for cyclists.

When I returned from my freshman year of college, in the summer of 1998, I asked my Dad to look at the bicycle I'd ridden around Pitt's campus. The hybrid was only a year old, but now that it stood upside down in my parents' garage in rural Vermont, it looked scratched and weatherbeaten.

"I can't believe it," said my Dad, "but I think we have to replace these brake pads."

I nodded, not understanding.

"I don't think I've replaced my brake pads once in ten years," Dad elaborated. He spun the front rim and squeezed a brake lever, but all I heard was a wheezing sound; the wheel continued to whirl. "You must use these *a lot.*"

And so it dawned on me: Pittsburgh is a city of *very* hard stops.

I lived in Pittsburgh for fifteen more years, and for most of them, I didn't drive at all. I rode the bus and bummed *a lot* of rides; but I also pumped my trusty hybrid all over town. And at every blind corner; rolling down every treacherous slope; through every blinking yellow light, I took my life into my own hands.

Pittsburgh was one of the worst-rated cities for cyclists, and many of its challenges are unchangeable. The streets are a maze. The hills are punishing. The pavement itself is cracked and pockmarked. Intersections are Kafka-esque. Even major roads are narrow and crowded with parked cars. Meanwhile, storms can pour for days, and freezing rain falls all winter. Gutters clog with jetsam; frost heaves rip open the pavement. Even the sidewalks are comically uneven.

In my memory, only true zealots commuted by bike, and they always seemed to dress the part: tattooed hipsters, flying around corners on customized fixies, flipping the bird at drivers as horns honked all around them. We were odd ducks, pedaling over bridges and cutting through alleys, narrowly missing side mirrors in our quest to get somewhere on time. I was no tattooed hipster, but the chaotic vibe matched the defiant headspace of my youth. I *liked* the danger. Riding untamed streets thrilled me to the marrow. Sure, I would've loved bike lanes and special signals, dedicated bridges and convenient racks; but these things were never going to exist, so I might as well accept the blow-by-blow threats of coma and paralysis. *Go ahead, Steel City. Bring it.*

Susan's accident changed all that, for me and for everyone. Fighting traffic wasn't a game, or a badge of courage, or even a statement. People could die. Someone *had* died. And not just someone, but an exceptional someone, a person so cool and beloved that her passing couldn't be ignored. The streets themselves were unsafe at any speed.

And for the first time, the landscape truly began to change.

New Directions

Morning becomes noon. I ride a rail-trail along the Allegheny River, passing woods and gray water. In the North Side, I find a network of bike lanes painted on the street. I pass a special parking platform for bikes, where attractive new racks stand in ranks. Some of these I remember, but so much is new. In the crisp air, I can almost smell the paint.

Noon becomes afternoon. I ascend a concrete ramp onto the Fort Pitt Bridge and coast into Point State Park. *Cyclists are everywhere*, zipping up and down the braided paths. I glide into Downtown, where I find bike lane after bike lane, the white lines crisply printed on the asphalt.

Like most urban networks, this route isn't a straight line; it's more like a high-speed scavenger hunt. I lose my way several times, making awkward U-turns over sidewalks and parking lots. I slip between skyscrapers, zigzagging my way toward the next rail-trail. I spot a pair of signs bolted to a post: "Do Not Enter," followed by "Except [Picture of a Bicycle]." And I laugh aloud.

Don't get me wrong: activists have been fighting for bicycle safety in Pittsburgh for decades. In 2002, a rider named David Hoffman was deliberately sideswiped by a passing car. His story earned widespread media attention and support from fellow cyclists. Within a year, Hoffman had cofounded BikePGH, a cycling advocacy group, with Scott Bricker and Lou Fineberg. For the past twenty years, BikePGH has been a vocal champion of urban mobility. BikePGH created Free Ride, a bike-recycling program; printed the Pittsburgh Bike Map; and commissioned the installation of bike racks all over town, including on every Port Authority bus. Like so many American cities, Pittsburgh was already taking steps in the right direction, thanks to a feisty activist community.

But it's fair to say that Susan's tragedy radically accelerated the process. The Pennsylvania House Transportation Committee unanimously passed House Bill 140 in 2021, but anyone familiar with the bill knows it as "Susan and Emily's Law." The bill is also named after Emily Fredericks, a Philadelphia resident killed in a similar collision. In short, the law makes it easier to install bike lanes on urban streets. The implication, of course, is that Susan and Emily would still be alive if they could have ridden on this kind of protected pavement. What a difference a few feet might have made.

Not everyone likes the new infrastructure. Parking has always been awful, they carp, and the bike lanes make it worse. The streets are a convoluted mess of one-way streets and last-second lane changes, and all that white-and-green paint makes it even more confusing. Among politicians, bike safety is a favorite political shuttlecock. When a friend of mine recently posted a picture of himself riding his bike down the street, someone commented: "BIKE LANES ARE THE DEVIL."

I get it—they see another roadblock in a city full of roadblocks. I see a city that is finally taking its quality of life seriously, at least in a way that I value. But one thing can't be argued: Susan should be alive, and isn't.

In Oakland, not far from Susan's ghost bike, I find that long, concrete staircase behind the Frick Fine Arts Center. I heave my borrowed bike onto my shoulder, so I can carry it up the fifty-or-so steps. I did this hundreds of times, back when I lived in Pittsburgh; bikeable roadways would end, and I'd have to lug my frame up and down this kind of stairway. It ain't easy, but it's comforting. The 800-or-so outdoor stairways are iconic landmarks, a century-old accommodation for workers commuting on foot.

But then I notice something: a little picture of a bicycle, embedded in the cement.

This staircase has a ramp. I fit my tires on the little shelf; soon, the bike is rolling upward. To push a bicycle is so much easier than lifting it, and I marvel at this clever little channel. I stomp my way up, breathing hard. These are the little additions that make a big difference.

Understand, I would trade all these things to bring Susan back to life. Without question. The lanes, the paths, the racks cleverly shaped like the Golden Triangle—none of it will ever be worth losing her.

But I think Susan would have liked what Pittsburghers have done. The strides they've taken. She would be amazed what this city has achieved since her passing. Lives have been saved, more lives than we'll ever know.

I reach the top of the hill, set the bike down, and ride. And keep riding, as long as I can.

Part 4:
The Road Ahead

SOLE-CRUSHER

THE MRI is noisier than I expected. I lie here, perfectly still, and the machine hums, grumbles, creaks, and groans. I stare at the ceiling, hands clasped over my chest, trying not to move. One twitch or spasm, and I'll ruin the picture I desperately need.

I'm not *inside* the MRI. There's no blank white tunnel, and I don't slide into it like a human-shaped pizza. Instead, my left foot is clamped into a small box. Weights press down on my leg. I lie on the MRI equivalent of a massage table, staring at the ceiling, as speakers play the greatest hits of the 1980s.

"You're doing great, Robert," says Tom, the technician. He's standing in a little booth, and his voice comes through an intercom. "You know what, though? I'm gonna do that last one again. I didn't like how it turned out. Just sit tight, okay?"

I give him a thumbs-up.

"These images are looking real nice, by the way," adds

Tom. "Take 'em over to CVS and print 'em out. You can tell people, 'See, I'm beautiful on the outside *and* the inside.'"

I appreciate his avuncular riffs. Tom is a massive guy, like a bouncer in scrubs, and his speech is pure Boston. I assume he's made this same quip hundreds of times. Which is great; I need someone with a sense of humor right now, as we inch ever closer to a diagnosis.

The machine makes its cranky noises, and all I can do is lie here and think. What I'm thinking about is cycling, and whether I'll ever be able to ride a bike again. I can imagine walking with a cane, as weird as that would be at age 42. I could live with a limp. I could stand to stop and rest more often. I've already given up running and long walks.

But living without cycling isn't living. The bicycle means exercise, transport, therapy, balance. Riding down the street empowered me through childhood, a carless adulthood, and the COVID lockdown. On bicycles, I bond with my son; I socialize with friends; I go on vacation. I even write about cycling for national publications. Cycling is my bedrock.

All of this is at stake. And only this MRI can tell my future.

"I'm looking at these pictures," Tom's voice crackles, "and there's definitely something there. Don't tell the doctor I said so. She'd kill me. But there's definitely something there."

Yes, there is, I think. *But what, exactly?*

Night Attack

One night, about ten years ago, I woke up with a terrible pain in my foot.

Specifically, a pain in my big toe. The pain was sharp and severe, like a nail being hammered into the joint.

I tried to flex my toe, which only made it worse. I slipped out of bed and walked around. I was delirious, and the room was dark. Movement had no effect. The pain throbbed for hours, and I lay awake, tossing and turning, till dawn.

The torment lingered for days. Desperate, I went to the Internet, typing, "pain, toe, night." The results flickered on screen: these were telltale signs of gout.

Gout? I marveled. *Is that, like, a real thing?*

I knew the word "gout," but only as a funny-sounding malady. I had no idea what it was, and I'd probably mistaken it for "goiter." Apparently, gout was a form of arthritis; when a person's bloodstream contains too much uric acid, it can crystallize in the joints.

Which made me wonder: what the hell is *uric acid?*

Gout, I learned, is nicknamed the "rich man's disease." Uric acid is basically a waste product, derived from the same word as "urine." Crystallization takes place when body temperatures drop, which is why attacks usually happen late at night. Anyone can contract gout, but certain foods aggravate the condition—foods that, in the past, only wealthy people could afford. Porridge and pears wouldn't provoke gout, so peasants were usually spared; but red meat and shellfish made flare-ups infinitely worse, causing certain aristocrats to limp around their chateaux.

At the time, I had no health insurance of any kind, nor

did I own a car. My girlfriend dropped me off at a clinic called MedExpress, and I hobbled into the waiting room. When the doctor finally saw me, I described the symptoms and my own online research.

"Yep," said the doctor, scribbling into his clipboard. "Sounds like gout to me."

He prescribed an anti-inflammatory, told me to cut back on beef and beer, and sent me on my way. Two days later, I was walking with ease. The gout might flare up again, anytime, anywhere. But for the moment, I felt only relief.

The Plot Thickens

For years, my diagnosis was little more than a funny anecdote. Friends told stories about asthma and diabetes, and I'd answer them with gout. Most people had some idea what gout was, or they even knew other people with the same issue. Gout was a harmless topic. It didn't have the gravitas of, say, Celiac disease or fibromyalgia. Gout was weird. Gout was quirky. It was bloodless and invisible. I could *own* gout.

I could also control it in simple ways. My girlfriend—now wife—was already a vegetarian, and we never ate meat at home. Seafood is delicious but expensive, easy to save for special occasions. I transitioned from beer-heavy nights to wine-heavy nights. I already exercised whenever I could; now I had an ongoing excuse to exercise *more*.

Flare-ups were rare, and now I had medication. At the first hint of discomfort, I popped some pills and stayed off my feet, and the aches faded. I planned my doses around major events, like big hikes and long runs.

But the routine had its flaws: when a certain six-mile jog resulted in a surge of pain, I retired my running shoes. No more jaunts around the neighborhood. No more half-marathons with my wife. I would miss bounding down the tarmac. But as long as I had cycling, all was well.

Then I switched doctors. My new PCP, Dr. Sharma, made it his mission to downplay my concerns—*any* concerns, about any ailment. My formidable snore was not life-threatening, and I shouldn't bother with CPAPs or surgery. (My previous doctor had been raring to operate). Contrary to one nurse's theory, the blemish on my eyelid wasn't xan-thelasma—a sign of dangerously high cholesterol—but a simple sty, which could be treated with a warm towel. Dr. Sharma waved away my worries, which could be cured by eating fewer carbs and getting a full night's sleep.

And then he dropped the real bombshell: "I don't believe you have gout."

I cocked my head. "You... what?"

"You are not seriously overweight," he explained. "You do not have problems with alcohol. You do not eat too much red meat. There is nothing about your lifestyle that would lead me to believe you have excessive uric acid."

"But," I protested, "the pain in my toe? In the middle of the night? Isn't that, like, the main symptom?"

"This could mean several things," Dr. Sharma said in his unflappable tone. "And when there is an attack, you may use the same prescription, and it should work just as well. But I see no evidence that your condition is gout."

I left Dr. Sharma's office in a daze. I was elated, because I might *not* have a serious disorder that could spread and threaten my general health, as four previous doctors had agreed was the case. But then again, if I'd wasted eight years fearing something that didn't exist, what *should* I be afraid of? The pain could still return at any moment, whatever its cause. And if Dr. Sharma was right, then I had to unlearn everything I thought I knew—and start again from scratch.

Pain, No Gain

Of course, the worst attack came after a bike ride.

The day was sunny and warm, so I rode for two hours, along a route I'd never taken. The road undulated through the countryside. I'd affixed fresh new tires, and I decided to ride fast, something I almost never do. I stood up, pumping hard up the inclines. I ground my soles into the pedals.

The ride itself was pure joy. My speed broke personal records, and I whisked past fields and forests I'd never seen before. I coasted through an old mill town, where the road intersected with a familiar bike path. I love this sensation—of exploring nearby places, breaking new ground, learning how disparate routes connect. Twenty miles later, I barged through my front door, euphoric.

The pain came slowly, like the aura before a migraine. I started popping pills, just as my doctor prescribed, but the pain escalated. Soon, I couldn't move my big toe without squirming. The ball of my foot was untouchable. I hobbled around the house, wincing and grunting. For days, my only relief was to peel off my socks, lie on a mattress, and breathe deeply. Tears rolled down my temples as I whispered to the empty room, "*Stop. Please, just stop...*"

But it didn't stop. Days passed, and fistfuls of Ibuprofen barely kept the agony at bay. I pressed ice packs against my sole, avoided all socks and shoes, and invested in a "booty."

Still, the pain persisted, day and night, like an endless corkscrew twisting into my flesh.

At last, I relented. I would call a specialist. Whatever my affliction, I must find its cause. And treat it, no matter what the price—even if it meant never riding a bike again.

The Toe Bone's Connected to the Sesamoid

"The good news is, it's definitely not gout," declares Dr. Sousa, my new podiatrist. She holds an X-ray to the light and points at my lower foot. "These are your sesamoid bones. You have two in each foot, adjacent to your metatarsals."

I squint at the image. The sesamoids are tiny, perhaps the size of two chickpeas. They look so trivial, compared to the matrix of bones that surround them. Even the name sounds silly; I imagine a children's show about extraterrestrials called *Sesamoid Street.*

"As you can see," Dr. Sousa continues, "one of those sesamoid bones does not look healthy. You see how it's gray and sort of shapeless? That *could* be because the bone has experienced a stress fracture. But it's difficult to tell from this X-ray. I want you to do an MRI, just so we can have a clearer picture of what's going on."

A stress fracture, I think. *But when? How? I've had flare-ups for 10 years. What was I doing a decade ago that might have cracked this little bonelet in half?*

No matter. In a few days, I will submit myself to the MRI. A week after that, I'll finally find out what the hell was wrong with me.

My mind reels. For so many people, foot pain is merely inconvenient. But for me—a native Vermonter, a passionate outdoorsman—foot pain is an all-consuming curse. I love to tromp around the woods with my son, in any weather. I love to run and climb and wade into water. And I love, more than almost anything in life, to hop on a bike saddle and ride.

A chronic foot problem threatens it all. I could operate a bicycle with one hand, or one eye, or one kidney. But I need both feet to push the pedals. Our feet are our foundation. Without our feet, medical science must go to great lengths—wheelchairs, prosthetics—to mobilize our bodies. A cyclist with a foot injury is a sadistic twist of fate, like Beethoven losing his hearing, or Degas losing his sight.

Which is a tough pill to swallow.

But there's a much bigger pill, which must be choked down: I'm now middle-aged.

My body has stopped being young. My twenties and thirties are behind me, and I can no longer feel indestructible. I can't shrug off regular check-ups, as so many young males do. Yes, I've withstood athletic abuse for years; but now, suddenly, I can't. Wounds won't just heal. Aches will linger. Belly fat is harder to shed. I've never given much thought to blood clots and skin cancer, bad knees and colonoscopies, but now I have to. The thousand natural shocks are catching up with me. Just like that, I'm basically kind of old.

The bicycle has always been my insurance against old age. I could give up all sorts of physical pastimes, but not cycling. I imagine cranking the pedals long into my golden years. Plenty of septuagenarians still ride their bikes crosscountry, and damn it, so will I.

Except—what if I can't? What if it's physically impossible? What kind of person will I be without the ability to pedal, let alone walk? I think about my last ride through the New England countryside, the freedom I felt, and the near-biblical punishment that followed. Should I expect every little excursion to result in debilitating pain?

I lie down and take a breath. That's all I can do, for now.

I fire up my laptop and type a search into Google. Seconds later, my screen is plastered with images—of hand-cycles. Athletes sit in recumbent seats, their fingers wrapped around hand-cranks. As they turn the device with their arms, these aerodynamic tricycles are propelled down the pavement.

Hand-cycles were engineered for riders with spine injuries and degenerative diseases. I don't have paraplegia, of course, and I would never compare my condition to theirs. But a hand-cycle is still an option. And this knowledge soothes me. One way or another, I will ride again, and on into my twilight years. There's a gadget for everything, and this could be mine.

I try to imagine it, flexing my way forward with biceps instead of thighs. This new form of exercise would take practice, conditioning, trial and error.

But my God, I'd be ripped.

I could deal with that, I think. *Being ripped. Maybe this won't be so bad after all.*

Sticks and Stones

"The bone is definitely broken," says Dr. Sousa. "The MRI was very clear. But you have two options: a cortisone shot may be all you need. Or we can remove it."

In a matter of minutes, my terror fades. The bone can be removed. The surgery is routine and will take less than an hour. Dr. Sousa claims I can leave the OR the same day; I can even drive myself home. Recovery should only take six weeks.

"You will have to wear an ugly padded shoe," she says, "but I've done this surgery hundreds of times, and only one patient had any problem at all."

One step at a time, I think. *Literally.*

I opt for the cortisone shot, and Dr. Sousa agrees. I whip off my sock, lie back, and feel the needle jab into my sole. The steroid floods my tendons. And that's it.

Dr. Sousa advises me to order a small orthotic pad, which I can stick to the bottom of my foot. The pad is shaped like a lily leaf and made of gel; it feels like stepping in warm mud, and it works like a charm. None of these are surefire solutions; the cortisone could wear off, and surgery may still be the best plan. But for now, I can stand on my own two feet, and that's all that matters.

The Road to Recovery

My first ride is short, just a three-mile loop around Roger Williams Park. But I bring my son, who has waited weeks for this moment.

The air is sweet with fresh beginnings. It's spring, but cool. Sunny, but blotted with clouds. The trees are budding, but just a little. My son is eight years old, and I've never seen him ride so well. He dive-bombs down paths and charges up slopes. We laugh and jabber. We haven't really been apart these past few weeks, but neither have we been together.

This is our natural habitat—outside, wandering through the world. Like Dad, like son.

And I've heeded my warning. If I ever took my body for granted, I won't again. I don't know how to live without these moments. Come what may—injury, illness, global pandemics, whatever—all I can do is muddle through and keep going. Fate won't always let me off so easy, but I can only be grateful when it does. My son and I circle the park. We ride and ride, down the path, around the curves, and toward the rest of our lives.

Jumped

THE FIRST TIME I try to ride a Spin bike, everything that can go wrong, does go wrong.

To start, I don't have the family car this morning, and I'm running late for work.

No problem, I think, walking hurriedly down a riverside street in downtown Providence. *I'll just try one of these new-fangled Spin bikes. I mean, that's what a ride-share system is for, right? Short commutes to work when you're running late? And hey, there's one now!*

I download the app. I enter my credit card information. I swipe through the explanatory graphics, and I find the digital map. I tap the little bicycle that is closest to me.

The actual bike makes a sound. A futuristic, electronic *bleep-bleep.* It's now reserved.

I unlock the bike, pull it into position, and insert the end of the cable lock into its slot.

Big mistake.

The bike makes more noises. But it won't move. Panicking, I look over the instructions again. Then I see my error: I wasn't supposed to stick the cable back into its hole; doing so signals that my ride is over. Instead, I'm supposed to stretch it over a groove on the back of the bike, where it should snap into place. Now it's too late. The cable holds fast. I'd have better luck yanking Excalibur out of its stone.

But the app won't cancel my ride. Minutes tick by, which means money is being spent. Money for a bike I can't ride, for a rental I can't stop.

I frantically try customer service. Now I'm tapping out instant messages, corresponding with some faraway technician. I explain the situation as quickly as my thumbs allow.

For twelve tense minutes, I sweat and type and wait. Finally, the rental is terminated, and the bike goes silent. I'm glad the ordeal is over—until I realize I've been charged $4.57. And I'm *still* not any closer to my cubicle.

So, I reserve the bike again. This time I lay the cable over the back and start pedaling. The kickstand springs upward, and the bike jolts into motion. I pedal down the bike lane, propelled by the pedal assist. The bike coasts easily through a park, then down a bike path. I barely rotate my feet, and the speedometer reads fifteen, then seventeen miles per hour. The breeze refreshes my glistening face.

And then, for no reason at all, it stops. The pedal assist no longer works. What's more, it stops in the middle of a hill. An ebike without pedal assist is really just an incredibly heavy bicycle with limited gearing. I struggle to press down, and I feel ever more betrayed as the wheels inch up a never-ending incline. I finally dismount and push the bike into a decent parking spot, where I terminate my rental.

This time I've ridden for fifteen minutes. I'm another $5.50 poorer. And I'm *still* a mile short of my destination.

To complete the experiment, I hire an electric scooter, also accessible from the Spin app. The scooter carries me those last few blocks. By the time I arrive at work, I'm late; I'm soaked in sweat; and I've spent more than I would have on an Uber.

Still, I believe.

I *have* to believe.

Spin bikes will work, I tell myself. *Even if it kills me.*

Heavy Machinery

I forget, sometimes, how recent bike-share services are. I think of a municipal bike network as an obvious and low-tech idea; and yes, tourists have been able to *rent* bicycles since time immemorial. But "ride-shares," as we now know them, are only as old as the smartphone. There are so many things a mobile app can do: display maps, process payments, log time, and collect every data point of your ride. Every movement is tracked by GPS, making bikes easy to find—and hard to steal.

A few years ago, JUMP bikes came to Providence. I was jazzed about it. I knew how bike-sharing worked, and I'd borrowed bikes in several cities, so I was confident I knew what the city was in for.

Then I learned a surprising fact: JUMP bikes were *ebikes*. They weren't just dressed-up beach-cruisers with bright logos, as I'd seen in other places. JUMP bikes had heavy motors and powerful pedal-assist, and if you put enough force into your ride, you could accelerate to twenty miles per hour.

This gave me pause. I'd never seen a ride-share *ebike*

before. Did Providence really need such a high-tech machine? The city has some hills, sure—Brown University crowns a district called College Hill—but most of these slopes are gradual. Outfitting each bike with an electric battery felt like overkill. It was like calling a Lyft to take you to the airport, and the car that shows up is a Hummer.

All that changed when I actually rode a JUMP bike, one crisp afternoon in 2019. I downloaded the app and climbed aboard, and the moment I pushed down on the pedal, the bicycle whisked me away—along with all my hesitations. The sudden momentum startled me, but I was also delighted. What a feeling this was, to rocket down the asphalt with so little effort! Ascending Hope Street felt less like climbing a hill than riding an escalator.

I dismounted after a few minutes and locked up. Except I didn't *have* to lock up, because the JUMP bike was "dockless," which meant I could leave it just about anywhere. I walked away in a daze of mixed feelings. The ride was fun—*sinfully* fun. How was this possible, that I could rent a bike for a few dollars, careen through the streets without any exertion, and then dump the bike wherever I felt like?

Big Trouble in Little Providence

The drama started with an armed robbery.

The victim was an unnamed man in his forties. He was standing outside, in the city's West End, when a stranger approached with a handgun. The stranger struck his victim in the head. It's still unclear whether anything was stolen. But the details didn't matter. The point—the reason anyone cared about a random mugging—was the getaway vehicle.

The assailant rode away on a JUMP bike.

When the news hit, it sounded ridiculous. Who would use a seventy-pound bicycle, painted fire-engine red, to flee a scene? How did the suspect even use the bike? Didn't he need a smartphone, a special app, and an approved credit card? Couldn't the police just track the bike's GPS?

Well, no, actually.

A week before the incident, the *Providence Journal* reported that JUMP bikes were "easily broken into." An unidentified teen explained to reporter Madeleine List how vulnerable the locking mechanism was; a bike could be hacked in minutes. Rumors circulated that a rider could dismantle the onboard computer, so the bikes couldn't be tracked. This was a gift to thieves, and there was only one drawback: a hacked JUMP bike didn't have pedal-assist. The bike was free, but cumbersome—good for a joy ride and little else. Because JUMP had expanded so quickly, there were more than 1,000 units to choose from, standing on street corners, just waiting to be stolen.

In the weeks that followed, I could barely keep up with the *Journal*'s damning headlines. "Misuse of JUMP bikes a problem in Providence." "Police see increase in crimes connected to JUMP bikes." "Teens on JUMP bikes beat, robbed man on Federal Hill." And finally, in late summer, just a week after the West End assault: "Mob on bicycles blocks traffic in Providence, assaults people, steals snacks, police say."

Bad to Worse

By that point, locals were already grumbling about JUMP bikes. When the company first struck a deal with Providence, JUMP was known as a slick mobility startup headquartered in Brooklyn. But soon after Providence committed, JUMP was bought out—by a modest little corporation called Uber.

A year later, Uber raised its rental fee from $2 per thirty minutes to $9—a 350 percent increase. The backlash was vocal and immediate, and Uber lowered the rates to $3 per thirty minutes. This fickleness didn't look good, especially for a company that had received a $400,000 federal grant to install the bikes in the first place.

That wasn't all. The "dockless" bikes were turning up everywhere, "littering" streets and parks with expensive motorized vehicles.

All of this was bad news, whether you cared about JUMP bikes or not. But that last report—of 100-plus teenagers rampaging through Downcity like *bandidos* in a dime Western—was the final nail in the innertube. News stations called the event a "Rideout," a kind of two-wheeled flash-mob organized on social media. Adolescents flooded a convenience store and snatched items from shelves. One bystander was punched in the face. The stories of "hooliganism" were graphic and grotesque. And at the center of it all was that bright, red bicycle. JUMP had been taken for a ride.

On August 22, 2018, nearly one year after the bikes first appeared in Providence, JUMP pulled its entire fleet. A much-circulated quote came from Harry Hatfield, a spokesman for Uber: "Safety is at the heart of everything we do, and after acts of vandalism on JUMP bikes we have decided, in partnership with the city, to temporarily remove bikes from operation in Providence."

But the removal wasn't temporary. The bikes vanished, and their flashy hubs stood empty. Rain fell, then snow, then more rain.

New Wheels

Then, out of nowhere, Spin bikes came along. Spin—a company best known for its electric scooters, owned by General Motors. Once again, Providence stood out: my city would receive the *first* Spin bicycle system.

The arrival of Spin felt like deja-vu, but in a good way. JUMP bikes were red; Spin bikes are orange. Their logos both have four letters, printed in white on every frame. And just as before, Spin bikes are all electric.

As time has passed, I've warmed up to ebikes. They used to feel like cheating: too fast, too easy, too much technology packed into a machine that's supposed to be simple. But then I remind myself—not everyone is fit, or young, or confident in traffic. If you suffer from joint pain, you don't want to pedal a bike, especially up a hill. For so many, an ebike means *accessibility*, pure and simple.

Plus, bike-shares aren't cheap, so the faster you reach your destination, the less you spend. And the more short trips you take on a bike—so the argument goes—the more you use ride-shares for practical riding, not just sightseeing. Although that can be fun, too.

Spin has done well. No hijackings. No flash mobs. No price fluctuations. And people ride them *everywhere*. Walk around Providence on a sunny day, and you're bound to spot two or three riders gliding by.

So yes—I want Spin bikes to work. I want this system to last, and to make my city a healthier place. And if they're all ebikes, so much the better.

As long as I can get the damned things to work.

THE GLOBE-GIRDLERS

IF YOU ASKED to see my "bucket list," I wouldn't have one to show you. Nothing formal, anyway. Nothing written down or itemized, even in my most private journals. Whatever passes for my bucket list is abstract and ever-changing, like a game of telephone I happen to be playing alone.

But one thing tops the list. It's the most important—and most unlikely—entry, the one I daydream about with the fervor of Walter Mitty. This is the quest I never really expect to undertake, yet I'll be devastated if I never do.

I want to bicycle around the world.

The notion isn't as crazy as it seems. Many, many cyclists have circled the globe, ever since Thomas Stevens pedaled his penny-farthing 13,500 miles in the 1880s. A sturdy bicycle, well maintained, can take you just about anywhere, even places without roads. All you really need is time and money. And if you're clever, you don't even need much cash: Jin, a blogger from South Korea, only spent $5,000 per year during her round-the-world circuit—which is like one-quarter of my annual mortgage payment.

Indeed, I've read several books on the topic, and I plan to read many more, because nothing gets me revved up like a good round-the-world travelogue. I've read Fred A. Birchmore's *Around the World on a Bicycle*, about his travels in the 1930s; Barbara Savage's *Miles from Nowhere*, about her travels with her husband in the late 1970s; Peter Zheutlin's *Around the World on Two Wheels*, about Annie Londonderry's odyssey in the 1890s. There's something so pure about this goal, and I can never hear too many stories about it.

Most people don't have time or money, of course, and even if they did, they wouldn't spend it sweating their way down little-known highways. This dream is rare enough. But if I had a million dollars, permission from my loved ones, and no urgent obligations—like, I don't know, raising a child—that is exactly what I'd be doing right at this moment, and for a long, long time.

But there's one problem with this fantasy, which has dogged me for years. It all boils down to a simple riddle, which is easy to ask but impossible to answer: *What does it actually mean to bicycle around the world?*

Like, what route do you take?

And how do you know when you're "done"?

Full Circle?

Obviously, you can't truly "bike around the world." Oceans stand in the way, along with polar ice caps. No single belt of land is strapped around the circumference of the globe, so you can't bike in a straight line and expect to finish where you started. You *must* involve boats or planes, and probably several, to make the full journey.

Now, we *do* know the circumference of the planet. So you could always ride the *equivalent* of 24,901 miles. If you biked only five miles a day, every day, you'd cycle this distance in fewer than 14 years. But if you went all this distance in your own neighborhood, you'd be hard pressed to claim you'd "bicycled around the world."

So you have to travel overland, a long, long way. On that, we can all agree. But the continents have weird shapes, and any route feels arbitrary; longitudinally, you could bike across Europe and Asia, then across North America from coast to coast, and you'd convince most people that you rounded the planet. But you would also have skipped four entire continents—three of which are bigger than Europe.

Another way is latitudinal: start in Alaska, and ride down to the tip of South America. Fly to Cape Town, then bike north across Africa and Europe, until you reach the arctic regions of Scandinavia and the road simply ends. This way, you travel four (of the six rideable) continents; but you still skip Australia, which so often gets left out, and all of Asia, which is a pretty big omission.

Then there is the land itself: unless you're biking, say, Route 212 across South Dakota, you'll probably take a winding route through any country. You pass through mountains, valleys, and foothills. You hit private property and have to backtrack. You bike miles out of your way to safely cross a river. You veer wildly off-course to find affordable lodging. And so on.

I've stumbled into this problem on a much smaller scale: I tell people that I biked "across" Costa Rica. But I took a *diagonal* route across the country, from Puerto Viejo to Playas del Coco. There is a more direct route from coast to coast, which has fewer miles but hillier terrain. The two rides would have felt completely different, even if they both technically "cross" the country.

And what if you hit land that simply can't be traversed? There's no road? Or trespassers are forbidden? When are you allowed to just, you know, *skip it?*

The Ones Who Went

When Barbara and Larry Savage started their journey at the end of the 1970s, they flew from Egypt to India. This made perfect sense at the time; Iran had just been rocked by a revolution, and anti-American sentiment was intense across the Middle East. And that's not all: in her book, Barbara doesn't even mention the Eastern Bloc; readers simply knew that the Iron Curtain was impassable, certainly to a pair of free-spirited Californians.

The world is far more open now—give or take a global pandemic. But politics still dictate where we can and can't go. I don't expect to visit North Korea in my lifetime. Afghanistan wouldn't be a wise destination, probably for years. Even peaceful places like Turkmenistan and Bhutan are punishingly hard to visit. And COVID-19 has only made border-crossings more difficult.

But politics can also be abstract, even subconscious.

It's no secret that the Mercator Projection flatters the Northern Hemisphere. North America and Asia are behemoths, while tiny Africa and South America cower below. This layout has shaped our perception of the world since 1569, and it's been almost universally accepted ever since. The Mercator Projection illustrates exactly how European colonists perceived the world—civilizing giants on top, lowly savages beneath. Even Greenland, a sparsely populated island, is brawnier than all of Africa's nations combined.

I don't necessarily blame the map itself. Gerardus Mercator did the best he could, back in Renaissance Flanders, to flatten a sphere onto a piece of paper. But once we've spent a lifetime looking at this map, we make arbitrary decisions about which countries are important to visit and which aren't.

Of course, the opposite could also be true. I'm fond of the "South-Up" map orientation, which presents Africa, South America, and Australia as liberated land masses, dancing around a vast ocean, and the rest of the world as a squashed balloon.

The point is, we are biased by the maps we use. "Bicycling around the world" means something different to each of us, based on how we *look* at the world. Where we go depends a great deal on what we consider "home," and how we were raised to think about places that *aren't* home.

No matter how you do it, globe-girdlers have to cross enormous bodies of water, and you simply can't bike over the waves.

Since ships are pricey and flights are cheap, most travelers take planes. But if you're allowed to pass over tens of thousands of miles in the comfort of a jumbo jet, what other loopholes can a cyclist employ?

This question dates back to Annie Londonderry, who biked around the world on a hefty wager. Londonderry relied on trains and steamers, because the bet had never stipulated an exact mileage. She biked *in* many different lands—and a good deal farther than I've ever biked—but she didn't always pump her way *across* them, as the phrase "bike around the world" might imply.

More recently, I saw the gonzo documentary *Pedal the World*, by German filmmaker Felix Starck.

Starck bikes an astonishing distance, to be sure. But when he reaches the United States, he makes a bold choice: he rides the West Coast, from Southern California to Washington State; then he takes a plane to Florida and rides the East Coast, up to New York City.

This route is creative, and it's roughly equivalent to biking across the American heartland. (In many ways, this choice may have been even harder). But he *didn't* mount his bike on one coast and self-propel his body to the opposite coast. Starck interprets "around" in a different way. And really, when you've ridden 11,000 miles through 22 countries, what kind of douchebag is going to argue with you?

A different solution came from travel writer Simon Parker: he planned to travel *halfway* around the world, using a bicycle—and also sailboats. In short, Parker used only manual forms of transport, so no engines or carbon emissions. For many, a sailboat stays in the spirit of the bicycle: it's slow; it's labor-intensive; it's exposed to the elements.

My favorite route comes from Alastair Humphreys, an affable Englishman who biked from the United Kingdom to the Middle East, then across the length of Africa to Cape Town. From there, he took a ship to Argentina, then biked through South and North America, all the way to Alaska. He skipped Central America, but he also sailed a boat along its coast and had apparently traveled here before. Then he crossed Siberia in the dead of winter, an astonishing feat unto itself, and made his way back to Britain. It's hard to imagine a more complete journey, and like Thomas Stevens,

Humphreys needed two books to chronicle his backbreaking achievement.

But there's one final question: who cares? Most people don't. There's no governing body for prospective round-the-world cyclists, and you don't get a trophy at the end, only bragging rights.

In other words, "around the world" is a sentimental metric. It's entirely self-imposed. You bike really far, over several continents, and you spend a year or three doing so. If you do it right, you return home in one piece—and overflowing with stories.

I haven't charted my course, and I don't know if I'll ever have a chance to ride it. But I love the idea, and all the questions it provokes.

Like they say, it's all about the journey.

Sit Back and Enjoy the Ride

I remember the first time I saw one.

Not where or when, exactly. I was young, probably twelve or so. I was biking with my family, on one of our weekend excursions. The day was sunny and warm. I remember lots of trees around. And out of those trees emerged a bicyclist.

But he wasn't a regular bicyclist. He was lying flat on his back. High wheels spun beneath him. His head was propped up, like someone just waking from a nap. His face was lean and serious, as were his sunglasses. His legs pumped, but the pedals were propped up front, like a ship's foremast. The man seemed to levitate past us.

"A recumbent bike!" my Dad announced. "They're supposed to be good for your back."

And that was it. The whole event. Not much of a tale, I know. It took only a few seconds to forget the word "recumbent," and every other detail is lost to history. The rider didn't stop to chat about his uncanny machine; years would pass before I saw another like it. All I remember is my awe and surprise. That recumbent was like a mobile party trick, astonishing everyone it passed. How did the rider stay balanced? How did he even climb into the seat? What happened when he reached a stop sign? How did he look around? What if he hit something? And where did he even *find* such a contraption?

I also remembered my Dad's observation: *They're supposed to be good for your back.* I took this tidbit in stride. It made perfect sense. Biking is easier than running, but the posture can wear you down. I inherited my parents' Schwinn, a skinny road bike from the 1970s, and I never liked hunching over its curved drop-bars. I filed away that bit of trivia, and I remembered it from time to time. Teens don't give much thought to their spines, and twenty-somethings aren't the target demographic for chiropractors.

But by my mid-thirties, I had pulled my back enough times to worry my doctor. Somehow, when the time came to buy a new bicycle, that foggy memory resurfaced. And in a flash, recumbent bikes were all I could think about.

Well, not "recumbent bikes." I still couldn't remember what they were called. In my mind, they were just "those weird bikes you lie back on," and this clunky phrase is roughly what I first typed in Google. Not exactly a promising start.

Little did I know the bizarre chain of events I was about to set in motion. It started with a spark of memory, a flash of interest. It ended with surprise after surprise; coincidences beyond belief; a whole community I never knew existed. I would feel the impact of recumbent cycling for years to come—which is nothing compared to what happened to my parents.

The Unlikeliest Store

My Subaru rolled onto a narrow road. I saw the backs of houses and clusters of trees. The surface was bumpy, more like a driveway. I wasn't anywhere near the strip malls and restaurant chains that I'd come to expect of suburban Warwick. I slowed the car and double-checked my GPS.

This was the place, apparently. At the end of this road stood the official headquarters of Bike On. Here, tucked into a residential nook, was one of New England's leading purveyors of recumbents.

I parked in the near-empty lot. The building looked more like an office complex than a store. When I stepped inside, I found a reception desk, where a clerk greeted me.

"I was in the neighborhood," I explained, "and I was wondering if you had a showroom I could check out."

The clerk hesitated. "We're usually open by appointment," he said. "But since you're here..."

We stepped through a door, and a warehouse opened up to me. Ranks of recumbents were arranged on the concrete floor. They hung from the walls. They came in every color and shape, and each surface gleamed beneath fluorescent bulbs. I studied them, breathless, as the clerk summarized what they had available.

But they weren't bikes. They were *trikes*. The concept was the same—a wheeled, self-powered vehicle with a reclining seat—but trikes are different in every other way. They have three wheels instead of two, and they sit much lower to the ground. Their design is much wider, and they come in every arrangement: long, short, two wheels up front, two wheels in the back, large wheels, small wheels, skinny tires, fat tires, pannier racks, handlebars, side grips, and even electric assist. Some models can be folded, so you can stick your bundle into the trunk of a car. They look like a lot like Go Karts.

This, I'd learned, is what "recumbent" means to most people—not the floating dentist's chair I had spotted as a child, but a high-tech tricycle. And I could see why a trike would be tempting: the three wheels make it sturdy and easy to ride, so all you really have to do is pedal and steer. They're basically all-terrain vehicles, climbing through puddles and ditches with ease. Trikes aren't quite as fast as road bikes, but they move at a steady clip. They're remarkably agile, with a turning radius comparable to a regular bike. On the trail, trikes are the coziest conveyance there is, which has made them popular among older riders. Octogenarians with chronic pain and dizzy spells may not trust themselves on a bicycle; but they might ride all day on a trike, taking in miles of vistas and fresh air.

There was one big problem: trikes aren't intended for regular roads. Sure, I could *legally* ride a trike through downtown Providence, but I would require a flag in the back. This reflective triangle would bob awkwardly behind me, alerting cars to my presence. Meanwhile, trikes sit low to the ground, so every passing vehicle looms large. The one advantage of a traditional bicycle is how high they are; a rider looks down on most sports cars, and it's easy to make eye contact with drivers. A trike is barely visible beyond the hood of a car, rolling down the pavement at the same level as a baby stroller.

"Are you looking for anything in particular?" the clerk asked.

"Mostly, I just wanted to see what they looked like," I said. "But to be honest, I'm in the market for *two* wheels."

"Ah," he said. "Well, I can see what we have."

I couldn't believe that Bike On existed. The moment I entered "Rhode Island recumbent bikes" into the search field and hit enter, Bike On popped up. I visited the website over and over, browsing photos of every trike they had in stock. It wasn't quite what I was looking for, but it was far closer than I'd expected. Bike On shipped all over the world; customers—who made actual appointments—traveled from across the Northeast to browse their stock.

I didn't have to travel across the Northeast. Warwick was just down the road. In theory, I could visit anytime I wanted.

I also expanded my vocabulary. Bike On didn't advertise itself as a supplier of "recumbents"; instead, they used the broader term "adaptive cycles." These machines come in more varieties than I could have imagined: there are racing trikes, hand-cycles, and tandem trikes built for two. Some trikes sit higher, like rickshaws. Others enable two riders to sit right next to each other, like a buggy. The "OPair" connects a cyclist to an actual wheelchair. Bike On seemed to have an invention for every body type, no matter what the age or condition.

Get Anybody Riding

You may wonder—as I did—how a store for adaptive cycles ends up opening on an obscure road in Warwick, Rhode Island.

The owner's name was Scott Pellett. He grew up in the small town of Coventry, a few miles down the road. He was an outdoorsy kid, always poking around the woods and trails of rural Rhode Island. One day—May 1, 1971, to be exact—he decided to climb an old telephone pole.

"I was going after those old glass insulators," he told me.

These insulators were like green-tinted cups, and they had a distinctive look; today, they might be described as "Steampunk." It's easy to imagine how attractive they were to a 15-year-old scavenger. The insulators studded the crossarm at the very top of the pole. As far as Scott could tell, the old cables weren't used anymore. He shimmied up the wood shaft, until he was eye-level with the insulators. He reached out a hand—

—and was shocked.

"I touched a live wire," he said. "It was 13,000 volts in my left wrist."

By some miracle, Scott survived the electrocution. But he also tumbled from the pole and hit the ground. When he awoke, Scott was told that he had broken his back. He would never walk again.

"I kind of found a new identity," Scott told me.

Despite his injury, Scott stayed active in the years that followed—more active than, say, myself in my early twenties. In college, Scott learned about wheelchair basketball, and he became an enthusiastic player. He eventually married his wife Lynn. Together, they opened a fitness center, which they operated all through the 1980s.

But the watershed moment came in the late '90s, when he tried a "hand-cycle" for the first time. Scott was 40 years old, and he hadn't ridden any kind of bicycle since the accident. He had never *imagined* riding a bike again. Scott set up the cycle on the East Bay Bike Path, a scenic route that stretches seventeen miles along Narragansett Bay. Instead of pedals, hand cycles use a special crank, which the rider spins in roughly the same way.

"I still remember, to this day, leaving my wheelchair behind, seeing it get smaller," he told me. "I saw all these people, and they were so happy. There was this parallel universe, and I never knew about it. I just fell in love with it."

Scott used his natural athleticism to master the hand cycle. He told me about his first century, where he cycled 100 miles in a single day. A century is hard enough to complete on a regular bike; I couldn't imagine finishing it by hand. That simple crank had changed his life, and soon he wanted everyone to feel the same power.

What's funny about Bike On is how big it became. "I thought it would be a little part-time venture," Scott told me. But when he founded Bike On in 1999, it happened to coincide with the dawn of e-commerce. His first order didn't come from Rhode Island, or even the United States, but from somewhere in Israel. This single order was a paradigm shift; their website could be accessed anywhere in the world, and they could ship their units just as widely. Bike On didn't have to limit itself to handle cycles; they could sell any kind of adaptive cycle, modified to suit each customer need.

By the time I spoke with Scott on the phone, Bike On was nearly 20 years old. It had grown from an experimental side hustle into a 10,000-square-foot facility. His customer base was all over the map—seniors, veterans, families, folks with disabilities, living in every corner of the planet.

"Many of my customers have grown old with me," Scott said. "I've sold them five or six bikes over the years. We always say we can get anybody riding a bike, if they wish to."

I didn't buy a recumbent from Bike On. The trikes weren't my style, and their one bicycle was too unwieldy for our apartment building. But I kept thinking about Scott, and how one ride on a hand cycle had changed every aspect of his life. He had shared that strength and independence with so many others. How many miles had those customers traveled on their own, thanks to him? How much confidence had they gained, propelling themselves with their own muscles, like any other cyclist?

The time had come. I had to take the chance, test-ride or no test-ride. It might take some practice. I might take some spills. But I had to make it work. I was ready.

And that's when I found the Rocket.

Some Assembly Required

The RANS Rocket arrived in a massive box. The building manager called me from the lobby, clearly curious what was inside. I sprinted out of our apartment and tumbled down the stairwell. And there, in the back of our building's mailroom, a cardboard box leaned against the wall. It was the length and width of a medium-sized refrigerator.

I knew there was some assembly required. This is typical for bikes that arrive in the mail, but a salesman at Perennial Cycles had actually called my cell phone.

"This is just a courtesy call," came a friendly Midwestern voice. "The bike is mostly assembled, but there are a few pieces you'll have to put together."

The call startled me. In the anonymous world of e-commerce, it's perfectly normal to order an item from a website, enter your credit card information, and know absolutely nothing about the merchant. I hadn't expected so much as an email, much less a human voice on the phone.

The salesman assured me that I could call anytime for technical advice.

Now it was here, my coveted **RANS** Rocket, a used recumbent bike I'd found online for the outlandishly low price of $700. Like any bargain, the price tag actually made me nervous. The model was older, likely from the late 1990s. Both wheels were 20 inches in diameter, which is small for traditional rims. Unlike the model I'd viewed at Bike On, the Rocket's body wasn't very long; it could *just* fit in our apartment. Perennial Cycles had described the Rocket's condition as "good." The model had 21 gears and refreshed parts. The thing *should* ride.

But who knew? Aside from monthly rent and airfare to distant countries, I had rarely spent so much money at once. For me, the investment was massive, and on a device I had never seen firsthand. I would have to be patient, I knew. I must treat the RANS Rocket the way mechanics treat their homemade hotrods—as an ongoing project. Anyway, I'd already taken the first step: the Rocket had arrived safely. Now, I must put my Allen wrench to good use.

I dragged the box to the front entrance. Residents sidestepped the cardboard monolith as they came through the door. The apartment building didn't have much communal space, and I doubted management would appreciate me greasing up the lobby. Just outside, the property had a brick patio with a gas barbecue; most residents used this for picnics and parties. The space was empty now; I severed plastic cords, ripped apart staples, and the box opened before me.

There it was: the RANS Rocket. A candy-red frame half-buried in packing peanuts. My Forever Bike, just waiting to be built.

It wasn't that hard. The cables and chain were already

affixed. The gears were simple to mount. I easily screwed the steering column into place. The only challenge was the seat, which looks a lot like the recliners you'd find at your local swimming pool. The seat perches in the bike frame, and its back leans against a pair of stems. Unlike a traditional bike seat, which moves up and down, the recumbent seat can adjust for both height and angle. None of this had occurred to me, looking at pictures online, and placing the seat took me twenty minutes of trial and error.

I stepped back and admired my work. It looked beautiful, even better than I'd imagined. Now came the moment of truth. After all these weeks of manic research, *could I actually ride it?*

Like Riding a Bicycle

"Grab hold of the brakes," says the man in the video. "Because if you don't, it'll have a tendency to roll out from under you, and kind of an unstable, uncomfortable feeling."

The man in the YouTube video was Jim Baxter, the owner of Go-Bent Recumbent Bikes in Walla Walla, Washington. In the clip, he's standing on a cobblestone sidewalk with one of his bikes. He wears khaki shorts and a green polo shirt; his hair is graying, and he speaks in the cadence of a laidback uncle. Smooth jazz plays in the background.

"The first time you ride a recumbent," Baxter continues, "we like to do what we call 'the Fred Flintstone.' It makes it easy, and it establishes for you a trust that you can balance this thing. So it's a matter of just walking with your feet—" Baxter pushed the bike forward. "—picking your feet up, and then you just roll on the bike to feel the balance.

You need forward momentum before you get the second foot on...."

The video is just shy of four minutes, but it's packed with practical advice: hold the handlebars firmly. Don't start out on a hill. Don't lift the second foot too soon.

As I waited for my Rocket to touch down, I watched the video dozens of times. YouTube is plastered in helpful recumbent advice, but Baxter was the best teacher—at least where riding was concerned. Part of the video's appeal is Baxter himself; he's a husky guy, and his tutorial is so casual that he's not even wearing a helmet. You don't think of him as the successful owner of a specialty bike shop, but instead as a chill neighbor giving you a quick how-to.

This video was exactly what I needed, because—and I can't stress this enough—*I had never met anyone who had done this before.*

I rolled the bike into our parking lot. I climbed into the seat and gripped the handlebars. My feet didn't touch the ground, so I balanced on my toes. The handlebars felt loose in my hands; one little nudge could turn the wheel and send me sprawling. The pedals rose in front of me, along with jagged gears. The front of the recumbent looked like a saw blade, which would spin threateningly between my feet. I pressed my back into the seat, and I suddenly pictured myself as a test pilot, strapped into some kind of prototype.

I pushed off. My shoes danced over pavement. The wheels rolled. I lifted a shoe and pushed the first pedal. The bike rolled faster. I lifted the second foot. I squeezed the handlebars, desperate for balance. Rows of cars passed on the other side. I dipped into a side street, and trees and buildings scrolled past me.

I was riding.

The bike worked.

And it felt *amazing.*

All my worries blew away in the breeze. Yes, it was different. *Very* different. Every part of my body worked differently. But I embraced the new sensations. I could make this work.

It's like riding a bicycle. But it was more like learning how to ride all over again. I felt a primal fear, the same I'd felt in grade school, that the Rocket would simply fall sideways. I could easily picture a broken wrist, a bleeding arm. I hadn't felt this survival instinct for thirty years. I started and stopped, over and over, in that quiet parking lot. And then, emboldened by my lack of compound fractures, I turned onto the main road and merged into traffic.

The Virus Spreads

"So, you know how I was looking for a new bike?" I asked my Mom on the phone.

"Yeah? Did you get it?"

"I sure did."

"That's great. What kind did you get?"

"So—it's a recumbent."

"It's a what?"

"You know those bikes you lie back on?"

"No kidding! Do you have a picture?"

I texted her a picture. I was bursting with excitement, and I had to tell someone. The conversation resumed, and Mom was full of questions. Where had I found it? What prompted me to get one? How was it to ride? Where was I storing it?

"You know," I said, "it's super comfortable. You and Dad might get a kick out of it."

"Oh, I don't think so," Mom said, laughing. "It looks a little precarious."

"Well, not *this* kind," I countered. "But there are all these recumbent *trikes*."

"Trikes? Like three wheels?" Mom considered this. "Do you have a picture?"

I texted a picture.

"Oh," she marveled. "This is pretty cool..."

That's how it started. I didn't expect much of our chat. I was riled up, and I needed someone to share in my ecstasy. My first few rides had gone smoothly, despite all my fears. I figured Mom might enjoy the novelty of my story, like that time I went skydiving. I didn't expect her to take my suggestion seriously.

After we hung up, I received a text: Could I send her a link to Bike On? Mom wanted to see what these so-called trikes looked like.

More texts: Had I been there? Did I know what they had available? What was a typical price for a recumbent trike? Could they ship, or should they be purchased in person? Did I happen to have a contact over there, a salesperson I trusted?

I figured her interest would ebb. These were all natural questions, and they didn't mean anything. But the next day, Mom texted me again: she'd stayed up late, scrolling through options. She asked whether I preferred Company X or Company Y, brands I had never heard of. She wanted to know how the wheels should be configured for different types of rides. I scrambled to keep up; I hadn't given the trikes much thought, and I didn't think I knew anyone who had.

Then my Dad called. "Well," he chuckled, "I think you've created a monster."

I could hear my Mom in the background, laughing with hysterical glee. Now I knew—this wasn't a passing curiosity. Mom was hooked. She must know everything about these trikes, and she just *had* to try one herself. I recognized the same pedantic tone, the same obsessive quest for information. She'd caught the bug. Like mother, like son.

We corresponded for the next few weeks, trading tips and facts. Mom quickly amassed more data about trikes than I ever would. She found dozens of websites and reviews. She found a host of YouTube videos; in one, a plucky older woman recounts her many journeys abroad. "I don't go very fast," the woman concedes, "but at my age, I'm not in any hurry. I just want to enjoy the ride."

It wasn't just my Mom. Dad, too, had fallen under the recumbent's spell.

"They really make a lot of sense," he told me in his clinical tone. "I'd be willing to guess that traditional bicycles were only designed that way because of horses."

I reeled at this theory. Could Dad be right? Was the bicycle just a mechanical horse? If 19th Century gentlemen hadn't spent so much time prancing around on stallions, would they have designed the bicycle differently? I'd spent all these months thinking of regular bikes as the gold standard and recumbents as a clever alternative. But what if recumbents were actually *better?* What would have happened if, instead of the penny farthing, Eugène Meyer had invented the RANS Rocket? How different would our world look today?

One thing was certain: my parents were gung-ho about these trikes. I had drawn them into my cult, and I hadn't even tried.

Oh, Canada?

My parents have a talent for hobbies. My Dad is a skilled woodworker; he not only designed and built my childhood home, but much of the furniture as well. He loves to canoe, snowshoe, and cross-country ski. He once taught himself stained-glass techniques just to craft a window for his bedroom. He grows vegetables in his garden and taps trees for maple syrup. He loves to sing a cappella and perform in community theatre. Above all, my Dad loves to sail. He'd sold his sailboat a few years before, just so he could build a new one from scratch.

My Mom is the same way, and she often turns her pastimes into professions. She's fluent in American Sign Language and is routinely asked to interpret for people with hearing impairments. She's a voracious knitter, and she's been known to spin her own wool. Once, she won a scenic flight from a local pilot. She loved the prop plane so much, she decided to take flying lessons. Within a few years, she was a licensed instructor, teaching *others* how to fly.

Cross-country cycling is just one of their many pleasures, and they've logged quite a few miles. When I was sixteen, my family flew to Paris with our bicycles. We took a meandering route through the French countryside, across Belgium, and down the Rhine River valley. We toured castles and visited museums. We bought our meals from roadside grocers and stayed most nights on campgrounds. This is exactly the kind of vacation my parents relish—active, economical, and self-sufficient.

So it was no surprise when my parents announced their plan to bike across Canada. Their 5,000-mile journey would take months to complete—yet once they retired, they'd have nothing but time. The Canadian government had recently completed The Great Trail, a network of roads and paths that spanned the entire country. How better to celebrate their golden years than an epic ride across the continent?

But for the first time in my life, I was skeptical. Did they really intend to navigate the Canadian Rockies? Weren't there stretches of Alberta and Saskatchewan that were full-on wilderness? I pictured them setting up their bivouac in mosquito-infested swamps, stringing up provisions and sleeping with canisters of bear spray. It sounded dicey. Five thousand miles was ambitious for anyone, much less a married couple in their sixties.

For better or worse, I blindly trust my parents' judgment. If they felt they could schlep across the wild north on two or even three wheels, then I was the last person to stand in their way. I'd done my share of risky backpacking and always come back unscathed. At least they knew the language and terrain. And a trike might make their passage a lot easier; there was little chance of slipping on wet rocks or head-butting a tree branch. If things went south, all they had to do was—well, go south.

Anyway, my parents are meticulous planners. They wouldn't begin their journey for another few years. There was plenty of time to hammer out details—and gauge the dangers.

What Are the Odds?

Then it happened. One of the strangest coincidences I've ever heard of. A sign—if you believe in that kind of thing—that they were on the right track.

Mom went to Google. She typed "recumbent bikes Vermont" into the search field.

A map materialized, outlining the borders of her home state. Several bike shops popped up, pinned to digital landmarks. Mom scanned the familiar names, until she found one she'd never seen before.

RAD Innovations.

She clicked on the link; a website emerged. The heading read: ADAPTIVE BIKES FOR ALL ABILITIES. Beneath ran a list of different types: recumbent trikes, tandem bikes, hand cycles, adaptive pushchairs.

That's exactly what I'm looking for, she thought.

Mom went back to Google Maps. She saw the address: 2170 Route 125, Cornwall, VT.

Cornwall. Her own town.

A town with only 1,000 people and not a single gas station. The same place my parents had lived for 40 years; where they had built their house; where my Dad had taught sixth grade and volunteered for the local fire department. The kind of town where "everybody knows everybody."

Somehow, they'd had no idea that a major bike retailer was located *only a few miles from their front door*. And not just any bike retailer, but a business that specialized in adaptive trikes, the very thing she had just decided to look for. RAD was practically around the corner. Given some free time and good weather, she could theoretically walk there.

Mom called the number. She was giddy. A woman

picked up, and Mom blurted, "Are you really in Cornwall, Vermont?"

There was a pause.

"Yes," said the voice on the receiver. "Who is this?"

RADical Thinking

RAD Innovations didn't have a storefront. No sign was visible from the road. At the end of a long driveway, my parents pulled up to a traditional Vermont farm, complete with barns, an old silo, and grazing livestock.

The woman on the phone was Anja Wrede, who co-owned RAD with her husband David Black. Anja was a sturdy German woman with glasses and a ponytail; David had a silver mop and a wrestler's build. They lived on the farm together, raised livestock, and hosted visitors in their guesthouse—all classic Vermont pursuits. But there was something else: the on-site workshop for adaptive cycles.

As my parents soon learned, they weren't RAD's usual customers. Anja and David sold all kinds of cycles, but their target market was people with actual disabilities. They sold hand cycles to riders with spinal injuries. They sold special tandems to people with seeing impairments. They sold "running frames" to people with cerebral palsy. As RAD's solitary mechanic, Anja could outfit a cycle for almost any condition: Parkinson's, amputations, balance issues, whatever. Only a small minority—maybe twenty percent—just needed an easier ride.

"There are Baby Boomers who want to stay active, but they can't risk the fall," David told me later. "I've got cases where they can do certain things now that they won't be able to do too far out from now."

Anja and David had each embarked on long and winding journeys before they found each other. David grew up in Northern Virginia, but when his father became an early Peace Corps volunteer, David spent two adolescent years in Kenya. He developed a passion for horses, which continues to this day. After a long and storied IT career, David spent much of the '90s developing adult pushchairs and running strollers. David was an engineer by trade, and he was drawn to industrial design. He wasn't a serious cyclist.

In contrast, Anja grew up in the city of Potsdam, which was then in East Germany. She was twenty years old when the Berlin Wall came down; until then, she had trained as a mason. Once the nation was united, a formerly West German bike shop needed some tile work done; the owners offered to build Anja a bicycle in lieu of cash payment. Soon, she was working for the shop herself, commuting back and forth by bike.

"I worked there for about a year," she told me. In 1991, she joined another bike shop, this time as a business partner. "We had this bike shop for a while, and that was when I was an avid bike rider. We would go with friends to Mallorca and ride a thousand kilometers in a week."

The pair finally crossed paths in 1999, when David made a business trip to Germany. Wrede was working as product manager for a bicycle company in Cologne; Black knew the owner of the company. As Anja remembers it, David "showed up at the office without an appointment."

They met-cute. They courted, married, and had a son. They moved to the U.S., and Anja became a citizen. After living for a while on the West Coast, the couple visited friends in Vermont, where Anja fell in love with the Green

Mountain atmosphere. So, they decided to settle down in the Champlain Valley. In—of all places—my hometown.

This is the kind of story I heard a lot, growing up. Off-beat characters from faraway places. Special skills and successful first careers. Bizarre pastimes that came to dominate their lives. Escapist fantasies of living a more authentic life in Vermont. Fixer-upper farmhouses in quaint little hamlets. Second incarnations as alpaca herders or artisanal candle makers. How many adults had I known, back in childhood, who had once been big-city attorneys and stockbrokers? My parents roughly followed this trajectory—suburban kids tired of tract homes and cul-de-sacs, who built their own house in the forest and taught themselves arcane skills. These were my role models, growing up. My parents' generation of drop-out Vermonters set the standard for painstaking weirdness. To this day, there's nothing stranger to me than not being a little strange—especially when that strangeness can help people, making the world just a little better.

This was the benefit of a farm, of course: it doubled as a destination. Fitting an adaptive cycle is an intimate process. You can't just click around a website and expect the perfect trike to arrive in the mail. David and Anja talked with customers on the phone, getting to know their lives and specific needs. When the time came, customers could visit the farm, stay overnight, and test-ride their new cycles on the long driveway.

"That's one of the things that's changed in the last few years," David said. "Beyond the idea of building and distributing a product, we are becoming more involved in the programs and the training of people wanting to utilize these kinds of things. That wasn't really on my radar five or ten years ago. And I love doing it. I like meeting with people and saying, 'Let's try this, let's try that.'"

"With some, we have dinner," added Anja. "Some come back as vacationers, and they rent a bike here and go on tours."

Third Wheel's a Charm

My parents bought two trikes.

I was shocked. I couldn't remember them ever making such a brazen purchase. My parents are famous—infamous, even—for careful frugality. I never imagined they would drop thousands of dollars on such an eccentric investment.

But it didn't stop there. With such unwieldy machines came the challenge of transporting them. Even getting the bikes home took some effort—stuffing one into the trunk of their Toyota and lashing the second trike to the roof. Car racks were useless, they realized. What they needed was a trailer. Or—why not?—new car.

This acquisition was even more radical than the trikes themselves: a two-seater van, the kind used for hauling cargo. Yes, they'd planned to replace their car anyway, but the Ford Transit was a sharp departure from the compact cars and minivans they had always owned. The van was eggshell-white and lacked rear windows. Despite the bright pallor, K. and I couldn't help but dub it the "kidnapper van." But the thing worked; my parents could easily store both trikes in the cabin, along with a mound of camping equipment.

By now, my parents had scrapped their Great Canadian Odyssey. There was no more talk of riding from coast to coast. That chapter was officially closed.

I was sad at first; I knew how long they had fantasized

about crossing Canada and how meaningful this trip might've been. It sent chills through me as well. This was an outcome I'd always feared—simply aging out of my dreams, no longer capable of the courses I charted in my indestructible youth. Selfishly, I mourned the loss of their adventure, because it was a reminder that I might one day have to lose my own.

Yet my parents weren't mourning. They looked relieved to relinquish such a massive undertaking. They no longer had to think about what kind of provisions to carry into the woodlands of Manitoba, or how many times they'd be forced to camp in a highway ditch. They'd never had anything to prove. All they'd ever wanted was the pleasure of movement. The trikes were safe and comfy. They were surprisingly fast and agile. They could cover fifty miles of bike paths in a single day. And in between, my parents could drive their gear from campground to campground, trailhead to trailhead, sampling bike paths across the country.

And so began their new journey—a 3,000-mile road trip from Vermont to Minnesota.

The Journey

They called it their "Great Lakes Circumnavigation." My parents set off from Cornwall in May and drove their windowless white van across Upstate New York. At each campground, they set up their tent and slept in cozy cots—bedding they could never have carried on bicycles. At first, the spring weather was unseasonably cold and overcast.

"Last night the temps were in the low 40's, rainy and windy," wrote my Mom. "A bit of a disappointment, but well within the definition of 'adventure.' It's funny how one word can help me adjust to challenging situations."

Every couple of days, Mom sent an email with their progress. The emails read like expedition logs, full of anecdotes, observations, and meteorological notes.

"The mall appears to be the amusement park of seniors, at least on Mondays," she wrote from a New York shopping plaza. "Fitness conscious elders were walking around the entire mall staying to the right, hugging the store-faced walls. Many moved with purpose, while others strolled. A woman vigorously waved to a man on the other side of the hall, who either had a hearing impairment or lacked good peripheral vision. He never noticed her. She, determined to stay in her lane, gave up trying to connect with him."

In Niagara Falls, they unpacked their trikes and took a spin along the edge of the misty gorge. "Our trikes garnered a good deal of attention," Mom wrote. "One family of three asked to take our picture. A few people asked us about the tricycles. Because they are still somewhat novel, everyone smiled as we passed by. Despite the cool temps, it was a great time to come to this famous site. No crowds. We heard Russian, Chinese, English, and dialects from either India or Pakistan."

The emails trickled in, narrating their drive through Ohio. The letters were full of Mom's eccentricities: wind-speeds logged in knots, precise distances between locations, notes on people-watching that read like incident reports. Batches of JPGs followed, showing my parents on their trikes, smiling in front of landmarks. Some showed only the trikes themselves, positioned before a sign or bridge.

They drove westward. The sun emerged. They hit more trails.

"Some rails-to-trails have different surfaces, e.g., grass, cinder, rocks, dirt, etc.," Mom observed. "The Cardinal Greenway had signs forbidding horses, but also one picturing an Amish horse and buggy with a slash across the image. 'No buggies allowed.' We saw almost 10 traditional buggies go by. None were on the path."

My parents arrived in Minnesota and spent a few nights at my brother's house. They visited playgrounds with my niece. When they started the return journey, my parents veered north, toward Canada. Mom ate her first Cornish pasty. They grabbed coffee at Tim Horton's. They used eucalyptus oil to ward off mosquitoes. They played mini-golf. They chatted up a waiter, who had recently fled Syria. The snapshots kept coming.

And they triked in Canada, too. They triked through an historic village. They triked along the Ottawa River. They triked over gravel roads. Each excursion was short and pleasant. This wasn't the epic saga they had imagined—but maybe it was better. Their passage was unhurried. Instead of the relentless crank of pedals, each ride felt like a reprieve from so much driving. They were never forced to wait out storms or bake beneath a blazing sun. They literally stopped to smell the lilacs. They had nothing to do but sit back and enjoy the ride.

"This evening, we are sitting at our KOA campsite, overlooking a water fountain in the middle of a pond," Mom wrote. "Trees are fully leafed, summer flowers are blooming, red winged blackbirds and bullfrogs are calling, with the ever-present white noise of the highway behind us. We are ready to get back on a trail with trikes... tomorrow."

The Road Ahead

One day, I'm biking down Pawtucket Avenue, toward my office. The road is a long, gradual incline. I've affixed a side-mirror to my handlebar, so I can see the cars before they groan past me. The road is noisy and hot. Yellow haze settles over the pavement.

I pass a bus stop. A handful of people are waiting in the shelter. They sit on the bench or lean against the glass. One guy stands out; gaunt, slouching, with a ratty sweatshirt and well-pocketed jeans. His head is shaved beneath a rigid cap.

The guy locks eyes on my RANS Rocket. His head follows my movement like a heat-seeking missile. He pulls his hands out of his pockets and flicks his fingers indignantly.

"What the *fuck!*" he exclaims. "Dude! What the fuck is *that?*"

The guy vanishes from my peripheral vision, never to be seen again. But I won't forget his face. Confused. Freaked out. Here he is, waiting for the bus on a busy street corner, and this random asshole flies by on some sort of doohickey. What kind of doohickey? Like a bobsled on wheels. Dude, seriously, what the fuck?

I stop at every red light, balanced delicately on my toe-tips. I'm pressed into my ergonomic seat and can't really look around. Cars vie for position around me. When the light turns, engines roar. I push the pedal as hard as I can, but the Rocket wobbles forward. The bike feels hesitant, unstable. I pick up speed, propelling myself down the street's narrow shoulder. I hug the parked cars. *Please*, I think. *Nobody open a door.*

Another red light. Another stop. The whole process starts again.

This is the first—and last—time I ever commute on the RANS Rocket. I love this bike. I love the comfort, the ease of movement. I love the aerodynamics, the way we slice through the humid air. I love pushing the crank-arms, the toothy cassette whirling like a radial saw. I love riding for miles without a hint of saddle-sore. I love the looks I get, the curious smiles, the questions shouted from passersby. *What do you call that thing? How do you like it? How much did it set you back?*

But recumbents aren't designed for cities, or even inter-sections. I learn this the hard way, of course. Starting and stopping are hard enough without dueling angry drivers. The turning radius is twice that of my regular bike. And when someone decides that I look ridiculous, I *feel* ridiculous. I try to shake it off, but the guy at the bus stop sticks with me. There's nothing you can say to *what the fuck*. I can't just stop and explain my Dad's theory about early bikes and horses. Nobody cares. When it comes to the judgment of strangers, there's a fine line between being a maverick and being a dork.

The RANS Rocket isn't the practical solution I hoped it would be. I ride it on the trail, for exercise and pleasure. But for errands, only a regular bike will do. Nimble beats snug. The truth is, I don't pull my back nearly as often as I once feared. Which is to say, I'm not *that* old. Not yet.

Yet every time I see the RANS, leaning against the cin-derblock wall of my garage, I smile. This bike has given me so much more than a way to get around. My family has be-come friendly with David and Anja; my parents visit RAD Innovations regularly for tune-ups and gear. One summer, I stayed in their guesthouse with my wife and son. We watched the sun set over the Adirondacks, and I took long-exposure photos of a comet in the clear rural sky. We would never have met, and none of this would have happened, if it weren't for those weird bikes you lie back on.

And there's more. My parents are still riding. On any warm day, they pack up their funny white cargo van and drive out to a trailhead. They pedal down the path for miles and miles, taking in the panoramic views. They talk as they ride. Recumbent bikes, adaptive cycles—they keep evolving to meet our needs, so that nearly every human body can keep moving, long after our legs refuse to run or trudge. To me, this is what hope looks like—something that takes us just a little farther than we thought we could go.

THE RIGHT SPEED

"Okay, let's start in the middle."

Snap, snap, snap.

"Like this?"

"Perfect. Now, when you start pedaling, it's gonna make a funny sound. Kind of a *clunk-clunk*. But you're okay. That's just the gears changing. Ready?"

"Okay."

"Here we go!"

Clunk-clunk!

Two bikes roll into motion. This road is flat, because that's the best place to start. Both wheels turn faster. Both riders pick up speed. The smaller rider changes expressions; apprehension, then curiosity, then excitement. This is nothing like that little-kid bike. This one really *moves.*

"There's a hill coming up. You see it?"

"Yeah."

"Try an easier gear. Turn it, so there's one click."

Click, click.

"Like this?"

"That should work. See how it feels."

The bike still moves at the same speed. This has never happened before. Hills have always been hard. Sweat and strain. Aching muscles and heavy breaths. Now the bike climbs at a steady clip.

"Nice work! Does that feel different?"

"Yeah."

"You're doing great."

"Are we going fifty miles an hour?"

"Well, not that fast."

"I feel like I'm on a motorcycle."

"I'll bet it feels that way, huh?"

"I'm going *so fast!*"

"Well, get ready, because we're about to go downhill."

"Oh, wow!"

"Yep. That means you go into a *harder* gear."

"Harder? Why?"

"When you go downhill, it's easier. So you can push the bike harder, and you'll go even faster. You want to go faster?"

"Yeah!"

"Okay. Click the other way."

Click.

"And again."

Click, click.

"There you go."

"Oh, WOOOOOOOOOW!"

And that is how the conversation goes. A kinetic breakthrough. Those toothy rings aren't for decoration. They *mean* something. Physics is at work. A bicycle is an elaborate pulley system, and riders are both operator and cargo. Riding a bike is no longer a matter of brute force; it's an art, mastered over the course of a lifetime.

This is me talking to Leo. It's also my Dad talking to me, and probably my grandfather talking to him. Sure, we all celebrate that first independent ride, when parent lets go of child, and everything comes into balance. But later come the gears. We're too young to comprehend the mechanics, and maybe we'll never really understand it. All we can do is *feel* the difference. We don't realize, as grade schoolers, the full scope of what we're learning, but it's a big lesson: we can shift our sprockets to match the land. We can adjust for our environment. We can help our machines harmonize with the world we live in.

Chain Reaction

The first bikes had no chain; the pedals were attached to the wheel itself. The mechanism followed the same logic as a Big Wheels tricycle, the kind you see toddlers riding around a driveway. That's why penny-farthings had such gigantic front wheels; to maintain a steady speed, riders needed that five-foot diameter.

In 1885, English inventor John Kemp Starley built an effective chain-drive, which made the "safety bike" possible, and the rest is history. Nearly every cyclist in the world uses some variation of Starley's innovation, along with every mo-torcyclist. The concept was so effective that single-speeds satisfied nearly everyone for the next 50 years.

Coastal Living

Leo pedals as fast as he can. He grunts and sputters.

"Leo! You're going downhill! You don't need to pedal!"

"I want to go fast!"

"You'll still go fast. Just stop and see what happens."

Leo's body freezes, but the bike still glides. The sensation makes him cackle with joy.

"*This is so cool.*"

"Right? That's called *coasting.*"

"Coasting? Am I coasting right now?"

"You sure are."

"Papa, look at this!"

Leo crouches low and leans into his handlebars. He's never heard the phrase "aerodynamics" in his life. This is not a posture I've ever demonstrated. There's no precedent for this. He just understands. He squints into the breeze, and as far as he's concerned, this is light speed.

The French Connection

In the whole cycling lexicon, no word delights me like "derailleur." The French spelling stands out on an otherwise English diagram: "pedal," "crank arm," "chainstay"—*dérailleur.* The French would pronounce the word "day-RAY-YOUR," but most Americans would say "derailer," which is exactly how it translates. The derailleur "derails" your chain, which makes possible the magic of "variable speed."

Even the cheapest bike has a derailleur, and most of us never even think about it. But we owe a great deal to this delicate little gadget, which hangs off the side of our rear wheels like a flexing robot arm. When we shift, one of the cables strung along the frame tenses or releases the derailleur, guiding the chain off its cogs and onto different cogs. Electronic shifters exist, but the vast majority of bicycles are as analog as they've ever been. *If it ain't broke.*

Ups and Downs

"Hey, Papa, can I take off my coat?"

"Sure. I'll put it in the backpack."

"I'm really hot."

"Yeah, well, exercise will definitely warm you up."

It's winter again. Two years have passed since Leo graduated from his balance bike. He's riding a brand-new model, a Christmas gift from my father-in-law. Everything about it is bigger, to match my growing nine-year-old. The tires are bulbous. Both wheels have brakes. There is no "ROYAL BABY" printed across the down tube. This is a Big Boy Bike, and he knows it.

We make our way around Roger Williams Park, up and down the undulating landscape. Leo never has to dismount and walk. He experiments with different gears, just the way I did, but he has keener instincts. I was hesitant at his age; I'd switch from the hardest gear to the easiest, inching up inclines and laboring across flats. Leo tests one gear at a time, easing into the grade.

Then we reach The Hill.

"Okay," I say. "Maybe we should walk this one."

Leo shrugs. "Why?"

"Well—it's pretty steep."

But Leo angles his bike. He's paused, but he has no

intention of getting off his saddle. The Hill is a walkway that drops down a grassy slope. At the bottom, the concrete path merges with a sidewalk, which crosses a small bridge. Ride too fast, and he'll lose control, or even throw himself into a well-trafficked road. There's every reason for him *not* to try The Hill on his first ride on his brand-new bike. I also know there's nothing I can do to stop him.

"Okay, hold your brakes."

"Hold my brakes?"

"Yeah. Not so you stop, but so you go nice and slow."

"Like this?"

Sure enough, Leo starts down the gray panels. I follow close behind, and we squeeze our brake-levers. Slow and steady. Like circus performers balancing on a rope. Halfway to the bottom, Leo says, "Can I just *go?*"

"Do you feel like you can?"

"Yeah!"

And he releases. The bike accelerates, faster and faster, toward the road. He glides into the sidewalk, turns, and crosses the bridge, as if he's done it a hundred times before. All I can do is try to keep up.

The Golden Ratio

Not everybody likes gears. Fixies and single-speeds pop up in major cities, and riders can be zealous. Fewer parts mean fewer problems can arise. Pedaling a little harder means burning more calories. On level streets, who wants to deal with all the bells and whistles?

"Nobody needs twenty-one speeds," says my Dad, one of his favorite maxims about bicycles. "You just need the right easy gear and the right hard gear. Those are the only ones that matter."

The older I get, the more I appreciate my Dad's perspective, and my cassettes have gotten simpler over the years. Still, I *need* multiple gears, and I don't care whether there are three or thirty, as long as I have options. Gears suit my riding, but also my personality. I want the ability to adjust to any situation. When challenges emerge on the horizon; when my body gets tense; when conditions turn threatening; when the journey is long and arduous; I want to know I'm equipped for it all—a heavier gear, a lighter one, whatever I need to keep going.

This is all I can hope to impart to my son: the tools to persevere and the practice to stay confident. So much of life can be like riding a bicycle, a matter of talent, muscle-memory, routine. But we could all use a little help. The little tricks and tools. The new habits and customizations. New roads remind us of old ones. Tires get patched and re-placed. Parts are tuned up. Limbs are stretched. Long distances feel shorter the farther we go. At the crest of a long hill, we almost always look back, surprised at what we see.

Go On

In the parking lot, I lift our bikes onto the new rack. Not a Thule, but a solid steel contraption that attaches to my trailer hitch. After a year of window-shopping, I finally bought one, and it works like a charm.

Leo jumps in the backseat, and soon I ignite the engine. We're both glowing in the rear-view mirror.

"Hey, Leo."

"Yeah?"

"You want to take off your helmet?"

"Oh, right!"

He unbuckles his chin strap and removes his forgotten headgear.

As I pull the car into reverse, Leo says, "Hey, Papa, can we do this again?"

"Absolutely. Anytime you want."

"Okay."

And if there's one thing I want in life, it's that he never stops asking this question.

POSTSCRIPTS

The World According to Thomas Stevens

Months after this essay was published in Longreads, a film producer named Sam Hartford requested my help in turning the Thomas Stevens story into a short documentary for the BBC.

Rein[forc]ing the Wheel

I used the Tannus tires regularly for several months. In the end, the airless tires proved too sluggish and I removed them. Improved tires and inner tubes have reduced punctures ever since, but I'm glad I experimented with Tannus and would try other versions.

Behold, the Kwiggle

After this story ran on Medium, it was republished as my first story for *Momentum Magazine*, where I am now a contributing editor. Karsten was overjoyed and claimed I was the first writer to really understand what he was trying to do.

He then sold me a three-speed Kwiggle at-cost, and I continue to ride it on local paths when the weather's nice.

Rack 'Em

I never bought an actual Thule, but the inexpensive hitch-rack I now own works like a charm.

Sole-Crusher

A year after the events in this essay, I experienced a flare-up of nearly identical pain in the opposite foot. This was confusing, because the sesamoid bones at the base of that particular big toe are undamaged. As if this writing, doctors still can't explain the precise cause for this inflammation.

Jumped

Spin has been widely successful in Providence. The company even has a rival, Veo, which has filled the streets with similar ebikes and scooters.

ACKNOWLEDGEMENTS

As always, I must first thank my loving family, Kylan and Leo, who not only let me write about them but support all my eccentric pastimes.

Further thanks go to my many editors, including Peter Rubin, Sam Hartford, Ed Simon, Elyse Major, and Adeline Dimond for first publishing so many of these pieces.

These chapters required the close attention of my writing compadres, Mike Kinnane, Abbie Lahmers, Alyssa Anderson, and Rick Claypool, who provide such tireless encouragement and feedback.

Heartfelt thanks, as always, to Nathan Kukulski for his insightful edits.

I must add a note of general appreciation, to the legion of cycling advocates, planners, engineers, maintenance workers, and mechanics who create these beautiful machines and gift us with places to ride.

Finally, I'm so grateful to Dan Parme for founding a press and seeing potential in this manuscript. Many miles to go, indeed.